I0759560

BUBALA

BUBALA

MIDDLE EASTERN-INSPIRED VEGETARIAN RECIPES TO SHARE

MARC SUMMERS

Photography by Patricia Niven

Quadrille

CONTENTS

Sumac
Sumac

Introduction

Food has always been my obsession. This wasn't particularly useful in my first career as a financial consultant, where my days were filled with PowerPoint presentations and spreadsheets, all while I daydreamed about tahini and falafel. It became clear to me that I needed to become a chef, to work in an environment I loved and where I felt happy to bring my work home.

When I'm not thinking about food, I'm talking about it and seeking culinary inspiration from both near and far. Creating Bubala was the perfect challenge for me. I have an immense passion for Middle Eastern cuisine and the hospitality that accompanies it, where generosity is key. I wanted to craft something unique, an experience that transports people away from their everyday lives.

The name Bubala (meaning 'darling' in Yiddish) encapsulates this feeling for me. It reminds me of being at home or at my grandma's house, where a comforting blanket of food made all the world's stresses melt away. No matter the time of day, you were always greeted with a fully cooked meal. My mum taught me that cooking for others is a way of showing love and devotion to those who matter most. I hope that sense of caring is evident in everything Bubala does.

At Bubala, I aimed to create a unique dining experience that reflects my love for eating. We start with a variety of sharing mezze – bread, pickles, dips, and snacks that kick off the meal with a bang. This style is typical across many parts of the Middle East. I fell in love with it. The next course usually features a larger main dish, accompanied by a side and a fresh, zingy salad. For me, this is the best way to continue the meal's journey – simple, tasty, and comforting. We finish with an indulgent sweet that leaves you feeling truly cared for.

With this cookbook, I hope you'll be able to bring a little bit of that Bubala magic and heart into your own kitchen – the joy, the boldness, the slightly chaotic energy that's fuelled us from our first pop-up to our latest restaurant. Play around, have fun, don't be afraid to mess things up. That's how we've always done it. Whether you're flipping flavours on their head or coaxing the best out of a humble vegetable, I hope these recipes inspire you to cook with confidence, curiosity, and a whole lot of love.

The Lightbulb Moment

Back in 2015, I was living in Sydney, having recently left both my job and my career in finance behind in London. I was searching for my next move, directionless and unfocused, sprawled on my sofa in Bondi when I happened to watch an episode of Chef's Table on Netflix, featuring the Argentinian chef, Francis Mallmann.

'You don't grow on a secure path,' he said. 'All of us should conquer something in life. It needs a lot of work, it needs a lot of risk.' Then came the line that hit home: 'So the message is, get out of your chair, sofa or office and go out.'

Was Francis watching me? How did he know I was lying there, completely stagnant? It genuinely felt like he was speaking directly to me. That was the lightbulb moment.

I jumped up, printed off my CV and headed out, handing it in at a few of the restaurants across Sydney. One of the most magical things about the hospitality industry is that if you show passion, people will give you a chance – that or they're just desperate for staff. Either way, it was a refreshing change from the world of finance.

After a bit of research, I came across a Middle Eastern restaurant preparing to open in King's Cross, Sydney. I walked in and offered to help in any way I could. Tom, the executive chef, gave me a prep role, with the launch just a week away. On opening night, the head chef walked out, and I was thrown in at the deep end with my very own section. The adrenaline was unlike anything I'd ever experienced.

The Roots of Inspiration

I embarked on a culinary diploma at Tante Marie Culinary Academy in Surrey. At the same time, I took a chance by walking into restaurants with my CV once more, this time at Berber & Q in Haggerston, East London. Restaurant manager Emilie greeted me and introduced me to head chef, Shaun. I was thrilled to be offered the opportunity to work as a commis chef alongside my studies.

Berber & Q quickly became everything I had never experienced in a job before – and I loved it. The open kitchen, the team, the vibe, the food – Chef-owner, Josh Katz and business partner Mattia Bianchi had created something truly special. It was very much a case of 'work hard, play hard', and it was everything I wanted to learn.

After completing my diploma and a brief stint at The Palomar restaurant in Soho, London, I returned to Berber & Q to learn all things front-of-house, starting at the bottom as a runner. I felt the same buzz as a waiter as I did in the kitchen. Connecting with customers and having the power to make or break their night was something I found completely energising. Seeing the way customers reacted to the vegetarian dishes was eye-opening and played a huge part in my eventual decision to open a Middle Eastern restaurant, that happens to be vegetarian.

When Emilie confided that she was planning to leave, I asked her to teach me everything I needed to know during her notice period. I was a waiter at the time and, looking back, I had no right to do what I did next: I met with Mattia and asked him to make me the manager of the restaurant. It may have been a crazy decision from a crazy guy, but Mattia offered me the role. I owe a lot to him for allowing me to take the reins, and over the following year, I learned so much; I was able to truly understand the world of running restaurants. Or at least I thought I did...

The seed of inspiration had been planted, and I was ready for the next step.

The Roots of Bubala

The idea of opening a restaurant where vegetables take centre stage truly struck a chord with me. Even though I'm not a vegetarian, the thought of creating something genuinely unique and pioneering in the world of vegetarian cuisine was incredibly exciting. My friends and family, however, were less than thrilled – to put it mildly. They saw it as a challenge, believing that cooking with vegetables was strictly for vegetarians and not something that could appeal to meat lovers.

What intrigued me was that the few vegetarian restaurants based in London at the time drew inspiration from global cuisines, with menus featuring everything from veggie burgers to curries and noodles, showcasing a world of flavours. In contrast, meat-focused restaurants typically offered just one vegetarian or vegan option, almost always a mushroom risotto or a goat's cheese tart.

It seemed odd to me that, despite the UK's great access to vegetables, nothing new or exciting was happening in vegetarian cuisine. I wanted to create a restaurant that was playful and somewhere I wanted to eat – it just happened not to serve meat. This focus on creativity has become central to what we do, making our approach limitless rather than limiting. The idea that anyone and everyone can eat at Bubala was a huge motivator. There is so much potential in vegetarian cooking, and many great chefs are exploring this space now, too.

The Bubala Pop-Up

Bubala began life as a pop-up. I wanted to test my ideas without the pressure – or the financial risk – of diving headfirst into bricks and mortar. Those early pop-ups taught me everything. When you're working with borrowed spaces and limited resources, you learn to solve problems fast, often with zero warning. That kind of thinking – quick, scrappy, and creative – prepared me more than anything for the rollercoaster of running a restaurant.

The very first pop-up was at Brunswick East, a brilliant Aussie-style café in Dalston, East London, where I used to grab breakfast on my days off while quietly plotting what Bubala could become. The owners, perhaps a little too trusting in hindsight, let me use their space from 4pm. We hosted our first-ever event over three nights, but after night two, I was told not to come back. We'd set off the fire alarm, left the building unlocked, and generally caused havoc. However, after turning up with two crates of beer and a sincere heartfelt apology, they let us see out the final night before (very understandably) parting ways.

Despite that rocky start, the buzz was undeniable. The first few pop-ups sold out, and I started to believe this could be something real. But just as quickly, I was brought crashing down to earth. Drunk on the excitement of packed venues, I sold 100 tickets for a space that only seated 50. My entire family came – mum, dad, aunty, uncle – and watched the whole thing unravel before my very eyes. You can't prep for 100 covers in two hours. You just can't. We started serving at 6pm, and two hours later, most tables were still waiting. My uncle had given up and left before a single spoonful of hummus hit the table. It was, fair to say, a total disaster, but it was also the very lesson I needed to learn.

Gaining Momentum

During this time, I started working closely with Tori, the then Managing Director of Gerber PR. She, very kindly, was helping us out for free until we found a permanent site. Tori clearly saw something in Bubala before I fully did, and that gave me the confidence to keep going. One day she called to say a chef had pulled out of a week-long residency at Carousel – a London venue known for hosting a rotating line-up of guest chefs. They needed a last-minute replacement, and I jumped at the chance.

That week changed everything for me. Emily Heron, an amazing Aussie chef, and I cooked five nights in a row, 50 covers a night, and sold every one of them. For the first time, we were serving people who didn't know us. No family, no friends, no favours.

Just real diners, paying proper prices. It was the most honest feedback we'd ever had – and it confirmed what I hoped: we had something special. It was time to go permanent.

Not long after the stint at Carousel, Emily told me she was moving back to Australia. It felt like a blow, but everything shifted again when I met Helen Graham, who would go on to become our first head chef. We connected instantly – shared heritage, shared love of Middle Eastern food, shared a vision. Together, we started developing the dishes that would form the heart of Bubala's menu.

Spitalfields: Our First Site

Later in 2018, I approached the owner of a shuttered restaurant at 65 Commercial Street in Spitalfields, East London. I asked if we could host a pop-up there, but they politely declined. A year later, I noticed the site was still sitting empty. This time, I asked if we could take it on permanently, and, miraculously, the timing worked. Within a few months, the keys were in our hands.

Spitalfields felt like the perfect home for Bubala. My grandfather had grown up just around the corner, and my first job in finance had been on Brune Street – only a 30-second walk away. The space was small, a little rough around the edges, but instantly warm and full of character. Within six weeks, we were open. And then came the chaos...

On opening night, our coffee machine overflowed directly into the electrical cupboard! No internet, no music, no ordering system. We went full pop-up mode: handwritten dockets, runners flying between bar and kitchen, a terrible speaker bought last-minute from around the corner. It was far from smooth, but we were open, and it felt incredible.

Bubala Grows Up: Soho and King's Cross

The Soho site represents a special moment for me in my childhood: when I was 17, I thought I wanted to be a chef. My dad had other ideas. For family birthdays, we'd go to Vasco & Piero's Pavilion, an Italian spot on Poland Street in Soho, London. One year, my dad set up a meeting with the chef-owner. I still remember exactly where I sat, and exactly what he told me: 'If you don't think about food 24/7, don't do it.' I took that advice seriously. I thought about food a lot, but did I think about it 24/7? Probably not – I needed some time to sleep, after all! So, I shelved the dream.

Fast forward to 2021. I read that Vasco & Piero's was relocating. I assumed someone had already snapped up the site, but with COVID still looming large, the restaurant world was moving slowly. I made a few calls and, incredibly, we secured it. I found myself standing in the exact same spot I had as a teenager, now ready to open Bubala's second home. A full-circle moment, if ever there was one.

Around 2024, Bubala evolved when Executive Chef Ben Rand joined the team and imparted his ideas, taking us to new heights. Then, in April 2025, Bubala King's Cross opened its doors – our most exciting step yet. With a wood-fired oven at the heart of the kitchen, we've created brand new dishes that give this space its own unique energy. Each Bubala site has its own soul, and King's Cross is no different.

Everything we've done – every misstep, every win, every wild idea – has gone into making Bubala what it is today: a restaurant where generosity, flavour, and proper hospitality come first. A place where you'll always find good food on the table.

Illustrations by Rory Downes

BUBALA
BUBALA

BUBALA

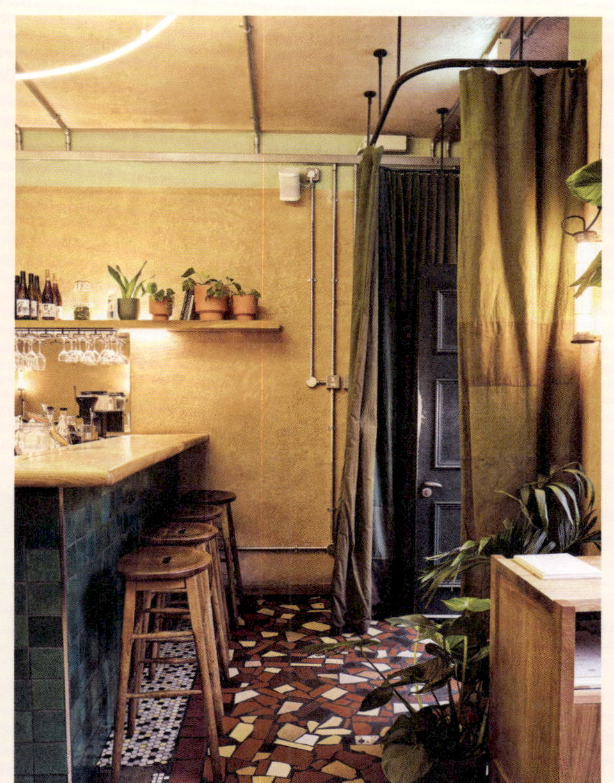

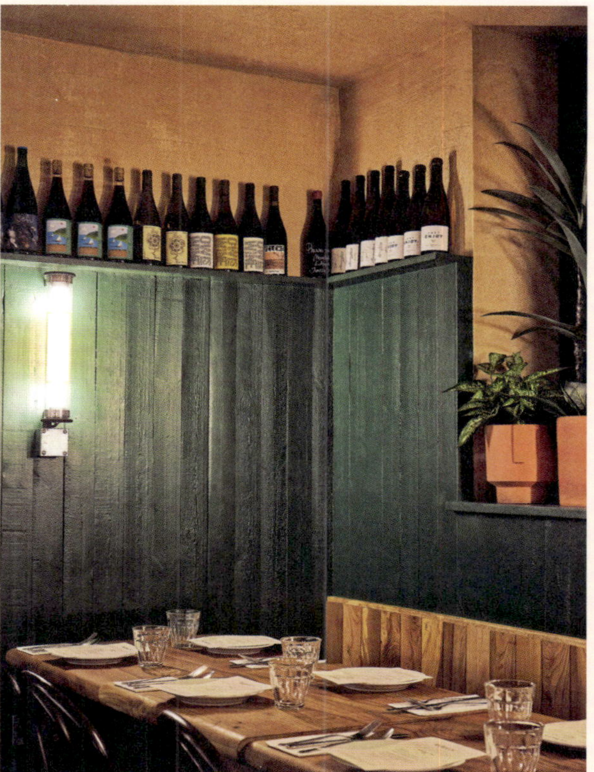

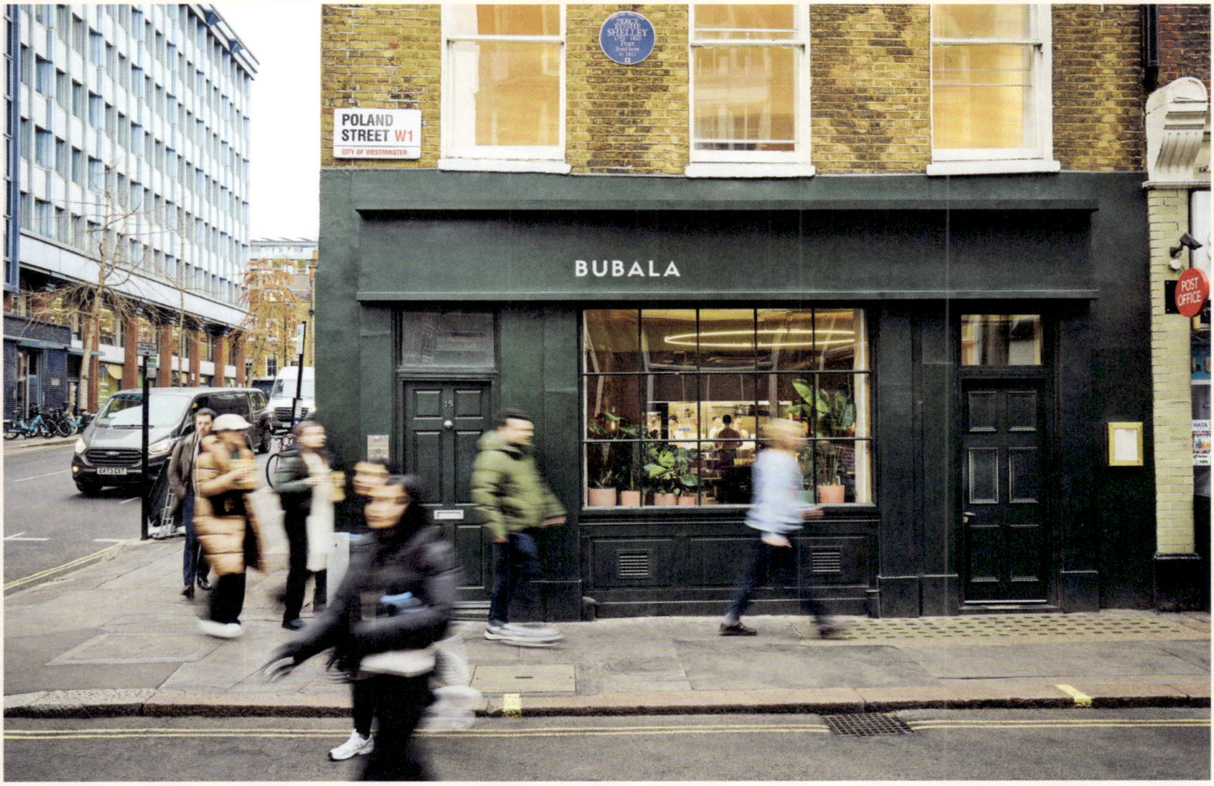
POLAND
STREET W1
CITY OF WESTMINSTER
BUBALA
POST
OFFICE

Our Food Ethos

At Bubala, our mission is simple: to show just how incredible vegetables can taste. We want our dishes to surprise and delight, to challenge expectations and spark curiosity. Each one starts as a playful idea in the kitchen, but they all must meet the same high bar: bold flavour, great balance, and a whole lot of heart.

Here's what guides every plate we serve:

Playfulness

Fun is woven into everything we do. We don't take ourselves too seriously, and neither does our food. We like to experiment, to push boundaries, to see what happens when we flip a classic on its head or throw in something unexpected. Our approach is instinctive, a little rebellious, and always full of joy. If it makes us smile in the kitchen, it's probably going on the menu.

Loud Flavours

Subtlety has its place – just not here. At Bubala, flavours are bold, punchy and unapologetically loud. We love heat, tang, depth and contrast. Whether it's chilli, vinegar, pomegranate molasses or miso, we don't hold back. We want every bite to wake up your palate – **hot, sweet, sour, sharp, spicy** – more is more. Every dish should be able to stand on its own. Nothing's just there to fill space. We always ask: if this was the only thing someone ordered, would they leave happy? Would they get what Bubala is all about? If the answer's no, it doesn't go on the menu.

Vegetables Are the Stars

Everything starts with a vegetable we're excited about. Maybe it's a whole cabbage, blistered and caramelised. Maybe it's chunks of roasted squash or a beetroot (beets) dip with unexpected depth. Whatever it is, our job is to let it shine. No gimmicks, no distractions – just big, beautiful flavour. At Bubala, vegetables aren't the side act. They're the headliner.

No Substitutes, No Pretending

You won't find fake meat or dairy substitutes on our menu. No vegan cheese, no plant-based burgers, no replicas. We're not interested in disguises, we're here to make vegetables taste amazing in their own right. Our vegan dishes draw on flavours from the Middle East and East Asia, where dairy naturally takes a back seat. Our vegetarian plates lean more into Middle Eastern and Mediterranean influences, where butter and cream have their moment. It's not about replacing what's missing, it's about celebrating what's already there. Real food, real flavour, and no compromises.

A Day in the Life of a Bubala Chef

The alarm blares at **6:00 AM**, and after a 20-minute battle (spoiler: the alarm wins), I drag myself out of bed. Coffee is essential, so I fire up a double espresso and brace myself for the day ahead.

I arrive at the restaurant early, just before everyone else. It's blissfully quiet. The extractor fan is off, the refrigerator hums steadily, and for a few golden moments, I can breathe in the peace before the storm. It's the perfect time to double-check that nothing exploded overnight. (Not that it ever has… but you never know.) Another great feeling is walking into the mountain of fresh produce that has just been delivered. Boxes of aubergines (eggplants) that will soon fill the room with their aroma while they're being grilled, or the smell of a delicious, juicy vine tomato.

By **8:00 AM**, the whole team is in – this is the best part of the day – and we dive straight into our morning briefing. We discuss the dishes of the week, who's making staff meals (a very important topic), and review the fresh deliveries. The kitchen's a whirlwind of prep, with our KP (Kitchen Porter) busy whipping up mushroom skewers that might just win awards.

Around **9:00–10:00 AM**, front of house arrive, coffee in hand, to set up for the day. We love them – they're great people and they help keep the energy up all day.

At **10:30 AM**, we make breakfast. Someone on the team has brewed a whole pot of coffee (legend), and we all sit down together to eat before the day really kicks off. It's a small but essential moment for connection: whether we're bonding over our favourite moisturisers or just catching up, it's the little things. By **11:45 AM**, it's briefing time again, but this time it's for both the front and back of house. We gather

around the bar to go through the covers for the day, including any large tables or rushes we should be aware of. We choose a dish and wine of the week that changes every Monday and use that as a focus for briefings. The kitchen team explains the dish, making sure to highlight any allergens and what can be removed without compromise to the dish. Front of house explains the wine of the week by going into regionality, grapes and tasting notes. This is a great way for both teams to expand their knowledge by learning from each other.

We then end the briefing with something called 'Question Time'. One of our managers, Holly, started this tradition and it's a fantastic way to get everyone ready for service. It could be anything from dream superpowers to bucket-list travel destinations or desert-island songs. It's something that really sets the tone for the day, gets us in a great space for service and has the added benefit of somehow bringing out all of the weird and wonderful quirks of the team.

At **12:00 PM**, lunch service kicks off. We have a cosy kitchen so there's usually only five of us, which is lovely as it ensures I have time to check in with everyone in their sections to see how they're getting on. The team is an amazing support system; we help each other out with section tasks and general caffeine-related support. We regularly have front of house jump in too, especially with making skewers as we get through hundreds a day!

By **3:00 PM**, the evening team arrives, and we do a handover, talking about what prep's been done and what still needs attention. During this time, the KPs are busy working on the potato latkes, which will be pressed overnight to create those perfect golden layers. Absolutely delicious.

Around **3:30 PM**, it's time for staff dinner. Someone on the team makes something incredibly delicious, often featuring potatoes, because – let's face it – potatoes are magical. It's the kind of food that recharges us for the rest of the day.

At **4:30 PM**, the team sits down together again for meal #2. It's like a family dinner, only with more carbs and less awkward conversation. We're all scattered around the restaurant with plates full of goodness. It's a moment to reflect on the lunch service and connect with both the front- and back-of-house teams.

By **5:00 PM**, the restaurant's buzzing with energy as we set up for dinner. The soundtrack shifts to Sugababes or Doechii. It's time for the evening briefing, where we go over the same focuses as the morning, with a second round of 'Question Time'. A wine tasting at this point in the day goes down much smoother than the early morning one, and the new cocktail tastings are always a hit, with the best turnouts. I wonder why...?

At **5:30 PM**, dinner service begins. It's our busiest time, but thanks to the morning prep, we're ready to go. Guests settle in for a slower, more leisurely experience, so we get more time to speak with them. As an open kitchen, it's always a treat when guests pop by to say hello. We're not exactly the most social of butterflies, but we appreciate the recognition.

By **10:15 PM**, the kitchen finally closes. Service is over, and now it's time to write the lists, do the stock takes and send out the orders. We have the best suppliers for the freshest ingredients – it's a great thing as a chef to be able to work with such first-class produce. The most important order? Staff food, of course. After all, we can't function without a good meal.

At **10:30 PM**, we dive into staff snacks. Yes, more food. After watching guests enjoy their food all day, we're definitely hungry. Latke offcuts, dips, and whatever desserts are nearing their expiry date – nothing goes to waste. And, of course, the bar takes care of us with cold drinks. After a hot kitchen, a beer is always welcome.

By **11:00 PM**, the kitchen is cleaned, and the front-of-house team is closing up the bar and prepping for the cleaners. The music turns up a notch with some Deftones or Chase & Status to match the energy as we wind down.

At **12:00 AM**, we change and head home. Soho is alive as always, even at this late hour. People are finishing dinner dates or regretting their pub sessions, and other shift workers like us are heading off, to or from work. No matter the time, there's nowhere quite like Soho.

Written by
Amber Neale
Soho Head Chef

Equipment

Grilling and Barbecuing

The grill is a central piece of kit in our cooking. We use Japanese-style Konro grills for their fuel efficiency, and the fact that they take up minimal space in the restaurant kitchen (and the models we use have a great shelving system, too). Using these grills means we can cook things hard and fast, while also giving us the ability to temper things and cook more slowly as well.

The addition of char or smoke you get from the barbecue is a key characteristic in many of our dishes, and something we have spent a lot of time testing and adjusting. Throughout this book, you'll see the preferred method for grilling is a barbecue, but you can also use an oven grill (broiler) if needed. This will affect the level of char, but it should still result in a really good replication of our food.

Measuring Temperature

A digital thermometer or probe is an essential piece of equipment in our kitchens, and we highly recommend adding one to your kitchen kit – for all sorts of cooking, but especially for the recipes in this book. It gives you accurate readings for anything you're cooking, but we really recommend it for testing the temperatures of oil for frying (see page 24) and testing sugar for making caramel.

We've identified which recipes require a probe thermometer in the introductions, and written alternative ways of testing temperature where we can – but a digital thermometer will ensure the most accurate cooking.

Wood-smoking

In a few of the recipes, you'll see an optional addition of smoking a particular ingredient. In our restaurants, we use wood-smoking to give our dishes extra depth and flavour. If you're up for it, it's a great way to enhance the taste of your food. There are lots of types of wood chips available, but we use apple wood, which provides a mild, sweet and slightly fruity smoke flavour.

Here's a simple set of instructions:

Equipment
Large baking tray
Cooling rack (that fits within the tray)
Large handful of wood chips
Foil

Method
You will need either a gas or electric hob (stovetop). Alternatively, you could use a small flame on a barbecue.

Place the baking tray over the hob and add a handful of smoking chips to one corner of the tray. Have the items you want to smoke within easy reach and turn your extraction fan on high, or open a window.

Heat the tray on the hob, concentrating the heat towards the corner with the wood chips. A kitchen blow torch can also provide direct heat to the wood chips from above.

As the chips get hot, they will start to smoke. Once they're giving off a consistent stream of smoke, drop the cooling rack into the tray and arrange your items on the rack.

KASAI

Quickly cover the whole tray with foil, to prevent any smoke from escaping. Turn off the heat and leave for about 20 minutes before unwrapping (and make sure you do this in a well-ventilated area, ideally outside). The food will have taken on a subtle, smoky flavour, and lighter-coloured foods may take on a slight orange hue.

Blenders

Our restaurant blenders get a serious workout. In most of our recipes we use either Vitamix or Thermomix – both of which are extremely powerful, and yield silky-smooth purées.

The recipes in this book are based on using these sorts of blenders, with blending times that replicate what we would do in the restaurant. A less powerful home blender may need slightly longer to achieve the same results, but we have described what to look for and how the end product should look and feel, where necessary.

Consider the times in this book as guidelines, rather than strict rules.

Deep and Shallow Frying

In the restaurants, we deep fry at 180°C/360°F degrees, unless the recipe states otherwise – which isn't quite as easily replicated in a home kitchen.

For shallow frying, we've described what depth of oil to use and how to know when it's hot enough. We've also said which recipes can be shallow-fried instead of deep fried, and where it's really necessary to deep fry, to create the dish as we would in the restaurant.

Using a digital probe thermometer will give you a level of accuracy that's hard to replicate but we've suggested how best to test in other ways.

Sterilising Jars

If you're making any of the pickles and you plan to keep them outside of the fridge for more than a few days, then it's best practice to sterilise your jars for preservation.

Begin by checking your jars for any chips or cracks and discarding any damaged ones. Wash the jars and lids in warm, soapy water.

Then there are several methods for sterilization. The easiest, if doing multiple jars, is to use the oven. Heat the oven to 140°C/120°C fan/275°F/Gas mark 1, place the jars on an oven shelf lined with a clean dish towel so they aren't touching the shelf, and leave for a minimum of 20 minutes.

Alternatively, if you're only doing a couple of jars, you can cover the jars with cold water in a large saucepan, bring to a boil, and simmer for 20 minutes.

You can also sterilise jars in the dishwasher by placing the glass jars on the rinse cycle, at the hottest temperature, without detergent, and fill them while still warm.

Lemon + Fennel
cucumber PICK ZA 22/3
ROMANESCO
STRAWB SYRUP
STRAWBERRY
cucumber PICK ZA 22/3

How to Use this Book

Bubala is all about feasting and sharing. Our dishes are designed to work together and bring something different to the table, collectively. In our restaurants, we champion set menus built around the notions of sharing and feasting – and the recipes in this book should be approached in the same vein.

Bubala Knows Best

At our restaurants, the Bubala Knows Best set menus, suitable for vegetarians or vegans, are the best way to get to know our cooking. You start with pickles, then dips and laffa flatbreads, before moving on to snacks and skewers followed by mains and sides. It's the perfect journey through our kitchen and showcases all that our restaurants have to offer. By the end of this abundance of delicious food, you'll be comfortably full – just as I used to be, visiting my grandma's house, which is the essence of what I have tried to replicate at Bubala.

Now, there's no need to cook a full 10–12 dishes to enjoy this book. While each dish shines solo, we recommend making a few dishes at a time to share with friends:

- 2 or 3 pickles to make a plate from the **Pantry** section.
- 2 or 3 dips, with bread and crudités, which can be found in the **Mezze** section.
- 2 or 3 dishes from the **Snacks** and **Skewers** sections.
- Pick 1 or 2 dishes from the **Mains** section, along with a **Side & Salad**. Then, if you have enough space, finish with something **Sweet**.

A Note on the Recipes

Many of the recipes in this book are **Vegan**. We have helpfully highlighted these on the pages with a V symbol.

BUBALA

Bubala Knows Best

Ararat Laffa Bread

Selection of Pickles (see pages 50–55)

Labneh with Confit Garlic and Za'atar (see page 60)

Burnt Butter Hummus (see page 71)

Halloumi with Black Seed Honey (see page 86)

Smacked Cucumbers (see page 111)

Oyster Mushroom Skewers (see page 118)

Romano Pepper with Mujadara and Whipped Feta (see page 133)

Potato Latkes with Toum (see page 194)

Endive, Orange and Walnut (see page 204)

Bubies

During the COVID pandemic, we briefly offered Bubala for delivery, but it quickly became apparent that our food didn't travel well. This realization led us to create Bubie, our baby sister brand, featuring a grandma as the logo. Bubie was conceived to bring the essence of Bubala to our customers while the restaurant was closed.

Bubie showcased the best of our sauces, vegetable cookery, and produce, all wrapped in warm laffa bread. This concept originated from what our chefs would make at the end of each service with leftovers, making it a perfect addition to our book for any remaining ingredients from the recipes that follow.

BUBIES

A *(Base)*	+	B *(Layer One)*
Hummus		Any Pickle
Beetroot Borani		Jalapeño Shatta
Baba Ganoush	+	Smacked Cucumbers
Labneh		Beetroot Fattoush
Toum		Sumac Onions
Tarator		

The idea is to combine one item (or more if you wish) from each of the sections below to create an incredible, filled flatbread. These are just our suggestions, so feel free to use whatever you have on hand. The goal is to craft something fresh, full of texture, heat, and spice: Bubala in a single bite.

C *(Layer Two)*	+	D *(Final Touch)*
Falafel		**Tahini**
Oyster Mushrooms		**Amba**
Halloumi	+	**House Za'atar**
Lemon Pepper Cauliflower		**Harissa**
		Chilli Crunch
		Zhoug

THE BUBALA LARDER

A Note on the Larder

So much of the cooking at Bubala is built on great ingredients and brilliant pantry recipes – of spice blends, sauces, oils and stocks. These are the essentials that underpin our cooking, and these blends and combinations are the secret ingredient to so much of the flavour in our recipes. It's worth taking the time to make some of the following recipes in advance of cooking through the rest of the book, to really help elevate your dishes.

Pantry Essentials

These are our essential store-cupboard staples, easily bought from most grocery stores and supermarkets, which we recommend you have on hand in your home kitchen.

Molasses

We use a variety of different molasses across our recipes. Pomegranate and sour cherry both offer a very sweet, sharp flavour to our dishes, and they have the added bonus of being an incredible, vivid colour.

The date molasses provides a concentrated date flavour that we use to create balance within savoury dishes, or as a more complex sweetness in desserts.

Agave syrup

We use agave syrup in place of honey in a lot of recipes, as a vegan alternative that also has a slightly thinner consistency.

Tamari

Tamari is a byproduct of miso and a gluten-free alternative to soy sauce, which we use a lot to offer a lot of the same deep umami and salinity as soy sauce, but without any wheat component.

Amba

A pickled mango-based condiment, spiced heavily with fenugreek, mustard and vinegar. We use amba as an accompaniment for our herby falafels, in marinades and salad dressings.

Olive oil

The backbone of a lot of our cooking, in our restaurants we use a Greek olive oil that is creamy, peppery and floral all at the same time.

You get what you pay for with olive oil, so spend as much as you're able, as it will enhance the dish immeasurably.

Vinegars

We use a range of vinegars – from fairly low-cost, simple ones for pickling, to more premium vinegars for dressings, made with single-variety grapes that offer very distinct flavour profiles.

The ones you'll see used a lot in the book are:

Merlot vinegar – a smooth, deep red vinegar.

Sherry vinegar – sweeter than Merlot, with all the nutty characteristics you find in sherries.

Moscatel vinegar – the sweetest vinegar we use, which offers a lovely sweet–savoury balance in dressings.

Tahini

The most used ingredient in our kitchen! We buy tahini in 18kg buckets and use around 150kg a week across our three restaurants!

This is an ingredient that really varies in quality, product to product. Seek a really good-quality tahini if you can that doesn't contain anything other than sesame seeds. We use a roasted version, which adds lovely complex notes.

It should be deeply savoury in flavour, with a natural sweetness from the sesame and no bitterness.

Pantry Recipes

Using many of the above store-cupboard ingredients, these recipes are made regularly in all our restaurants and form the foundation of much of our cooking. You'll find them used throughout all our dishes and the recipes in the following chapters of this book.

OILS & SAUCES

A punchy sauce or a well-made oil in a dish can pull everything together, add contrast, or deliver that final lick of richness. Whether drizzled, dolloped or swirled, they're small additions with big intentions.

Curry Leaf Oil

Makes 250ml (9fl oz)

4–5 sprigs of fresh curry, leaves picked
250ml (9fl oz) rapeseed (canola) oil

Fragrant, punchy, and vibrant green, this curry leaf oil brings a hit of South Asian flavour with minimal effort. It's our go-to finishing touch, drizzled over our Baba Ganoush in particular (see page 64), but can be used on any dips, roasted vegetables or really anything that needs a fragrant lift

Put the curry leaves in a blender with 2 tablespoons of the oil and blend for 5 minutes, or until smooth. Pour the remaining oil into a saucepan and add the blended portion.

Heat gently and simmer until fragrant, around 10 minutes. It will almost look black, or a very dark green. Take off the heat and strain through a sieve (sifter) lined with muslin (cheesecloth). Discard the curry leaves.

Cool and transfer to a sterilised glass jar (see page 24) and store, covered in the fridge. It will stay nice and green for up to 2 weeks.

Green Oil

Makes 250ml (9fl oz)

30g (1oz) parsley, roughly chopped
30g (1oz) chives, roughly chopped
240ml (8fl oz) rapeseed (canola) oil

There are no losers with this green herb oil. It adds further flavour to a dish without adding the herb itself, which can be great in dressings and sauces. It's brilliant for using up herbs, as well as onion and leek trimmings that are just past their best or surplus to requirements – plus it looks amazing!

You'll find this oil used in lots of recipes throughout the book as a final flourish when garnishing – in our Romano Pepper with Mujadara and Whipped Feta (see page 133), January King Cabbage with Shiitake and Baharat (see page 168) and Gem, Shiso, Hazelnut and Apple salad (see page 200).

Before you start, set a heatproof bowl over a bowl of ice.

In a blender, blitz the herbs and 4 tablespoons of the oil in a blender, then, with the motor still running, slowly drizzle in the remaining oil until thoroughly mixed. Transfer to a saucepan and bring to the boil on a high heat. You will see the solids separate from the oil. Once the oil is bubbling, remove from the heat and strain through a sieve (sifter) lined with muslin (cheesecloth) into the bowl (the aim is to cool the oil down quickly to retain the green colour). Discard the herbs in the sieve.

Transfer the cooled oil to a sterilised glass jar (see page 24) and store, covered in the fridge, for up to 2 weeks.

Tahini Sauce

Makes 500ml (17fl oz)

265g (9½oz) tahini
4 tsp lemon juice
½ tsp table salt

Tahini sauce is a remarkably simple mixture of water, salt and tahini. When combined, the water softens the intense tahini flavour and creates a rich, velvety sauce that becomes greater than the sum of its parts. It can be used in almost anything, but in this book, you'll find it in our Falafel recipe (see page 91) as well as a bed for the ezme salad to sit on (see Grapefruit Ezme with Tahini and Pomegranate Molasses, page 76).

Put all the ingredients and 240ml (8fl oz) of water in a large mixing bowl and combine using an electric whisk for about 30 seconds. The mixture should have the consistency of pancake batter. If it's too thin, add a teaspoon more of tahini and mix again. Check and adjust the seasoning.

Transfer to a sterilised glass jar (see page 24) and store, covered in the fridge, for up to 3 days.

Black Garlic Tahini

Makes 200g (7oz)

55g (2oz) tahini
50g (1¾oz) black garlic
1 small clove of garlic
2 tsp moscatel vinegar
½ tsp salt

Rich, earthy, and slightly sweet, black garlic tahini is our umami-packed upgrade to the classic. The fermented garlic brings depth and a mellow funk that plays beautifully with the nuttiness of the tahini. It's smooth, strikingly dark, and dangerously moreish – just the kind of sauce we want on everything.

Blend all the ingredients and 130ml (4½fl oz) water in a blender until smooth, with a pancake batter consistency. If needed, add a little more water. Keep in a sealed jar in the fridge for up to 7 days.

Tarator

Makes 200g (7oz)

40g (1½oz) stale flatbread
4 tbsp plus 2 tsp oat milk
15g (½oz) tahini
¼ shallot
½ confit garlic clove (see Confit Garlic, page 47)
½ tsp agave nectar
½ tsp tamari soy sauce
pinch of salt
3 tbsp plus 2 tsp rapeseed (canola) oil
4 tsp extra virgin olive oil

Tarator is a creamy, garlicky tahini sauce that's a staple across the Levant – simple, sharp, and endlessly versatile. At Bubala, we've added oat milk, tamari and leftover laffa bread, which takes this sauce to a new level. It's perfect as a dip for fried snacks, but also equally delicious with a plate of steamed asparagus.

Tear the bread into pieces and put in a blender with half of the oat milk and all the remaining ingredients except the rapeseed (canola) and olive oils. Leave to soak for 5 minutes, then blend until really smooth, adding the remaining additional oat milk if needed.

Slowly pour in the oil, blending well between additions, to form a silky-smooth, emulsified sauce, making sure the mixture stays smooth. Transfer to a large jar and keep in the fridge.

SPICE BLENDS

Spices, despite being dried, do have a shelf life on them.

For spices in the home kitchen, buy in small quantities, use regularly and replace as necessary. If possible, seek a specialist spice shop or vendor as it really will make a difference. At the restaurants, the coriander seeds we buy are a vibrant greeny-yellow and are twice the size of the ones you see in supermarkets, and the cinnamon sticks are noticeably sweeter.

When it comes to spices, we don't stick to tradition in our cooking, we blend our own versions. Inspired by Middle Eastern spices but led by flavour, these mixes are built to bring balance, depth, and a little surprise. They're a starting point, a finishing touch, and sometimes the whole idea behind a dish. There are a few key spice blends that feature a lot throughout this book.

Za'atar – a spice mix containing a wild oregano and sesame seeds. We've written our version of this below, but you can also find good za'atar in most supermarkets and cook shops.

Hawaij – a turmeric-heavy blend of coriander, cumin, cardamom and black pepper. This spice mix has a mild, earthy and aromatic taste with sweet undertones and a light, peppery aftertaste. We've shared our blend overleaf, but you can also find this in most good supermarkets.

Baharat – this mix contains all the spices I associate with winter: cinnamon, clove, allspice, nutmeg, cumin, coriander and black pepper. During the cold months it seems an obvious choice for adding depth to dishes, and it also works very well with sweetness – such as in the granola crunch in the Endive, Orange, and Walnut Salad (see page 204)

House Za'atar

Makes 250g (9oz)

4 dried black limes
45g (1½oz) dried wakame seaweed
35g (6½ tbsp) dried oregano
30g (6 tbsp) dried thyme
75g (8½ tbsp) sesame seeds
45g (5½ tbsp) sumac
2 tsp urfa chilli flakes

Za'atar can range from just a dried herb to a blend with sesame seeds in. We like to toast our sesame seeds, and then add the untraditional ingredients of preserved lime, for its sourness, and wakame, for a hit of saltiness. This results in an amazing finishing spice that we use on our Labneh (see page 60), and mix with oil to brush on our laffa flatbreads in the restaurants.

In a spice grinder or mini food processor, blitz the black limes and wakame to a powder. Add the oregano and thyme and blend to form a powder. Add all the remaining ingredients and pulse to combine, trying to keep these last ingredients as whole as possible.

Store in your spice cupboard in a dry, sealed container such as a glass jar.

Hawaij Spice Blend

Makes 325g (11½oz)

2½ tbsp cloves
90g (3¼oz) cumin seeds
45g (1½oz) coriander seeds
90g (3¼oz) black peppercorns
5½ tbsp ground turmeric
20g (¾oz) ground cardamom seeds (from about 6 green cardamom pods)

Hawaij is a Yemeni spice blend that doesn't hold back – it's bold, peppery, and deeply aromatic. Traditionally used in soups and stews, we love using it when cooking down onions to give them a deep flavour. Our blend brings together cumin, black pepper, turmeric, and cardamom for warmth with a kick.

Toast the whole spices in a dry pan until aromatic. Pick out the cloves and crush them to a fine powder in a pestle and mortar. Add the cumin, coriander and peppercorns and coarsely crush, then mix in the ground turmeric and cardamom seeds. Store in a sealed glass jar.

Ras el Hanout

Makes 240g (8½oz)

60g (2¼oz) cumin seeds
40g (1½oz) coriander seeds
4 tbsp dried rose petals
5 tbsp whole black peppercorns
2 tbsp ground cinnamon
75g (2½oz) smoked paprika

Ras el hanout means 'head of the shop' – a spice blend made from the best a spice merchant has to offer (Ren's Pantry in our case!) Warming, aromatic, and layered, it's a Bubala favourite for adding instant depth to vegetables, marinades, and oils. No two recipes are the same, but ours leans into cumin, coriander, rose, and a little heat.

Toast the cumin and coriander seeds in a dry pan until aromatic then grind in a spice grinder or mortar and pestle. Grind the rose petals and black pepper, then add the remaining ingredients and combine everything together. Transfer to a clean glass jar and seal well.

Harissa Salt

Makes about 350g (12oz)

2½ tsp coriander seeds
2½ tsp cumin seeds
2½ tsp caraway seeds
1 tsp cracked black pepper
1 tsp smoked paprika
2 dried bay leaves
350g (12oz) fine salt

We took all the dry spices traditionally found in harissa, toasted them, ground them to a powder and mixed them through salt. This is a great way to impart further flavours into vegetables. In our kitchens, we use this for dry-brining, which pulls moisture out of vegetables like courgettes (zucchini), and then they take on the spices in the salt. It's a great way to add an extra layer of complexity into our dishes.

Toast the coriander, cumin and caraway seeds in a dry pan until golden and fragrant, then crush in a pestle and mortar. Combine with the cracked black pepper, paprika and bay leaves, then mix in the salt until evenly combined. Store in a sealed glass jar.

Sesame Crumb

Makes about 50g (1⅜oz)

2½ tbsp white sesame seeds
2½ tbsp black sesame seeds
2 tsp smoked paprika
½ tsp flaky sea salt
½ tsp soft brown sugar

A salty, sweet, smoky seasoning. A great way to finish seasoning vegetables with more than just salt, and it looks great too! You'll find this in our Friggitelli Peppers (see page 95) and our Beetroot with Black Garlic Tahini (see page 134).

Toast both types of sesame seeds in a dry frying pan (skillet) until fragrant. Allow to cool a little, then transfer to a blender with all the other ingredients and pulse just until roughly blitzed. Store in a sealed glass jar in your pantry or store cupboard.

STOCKS

Stocks are the unsung heroes of our kitchen: subtle, soulful, and full of depth. We use them to build flavour gently, letting vegetables shine while adding warmth and complexity. Made from simple ingredients – often scraps and trimmings – our stocks are low-waste, high-reward, and quietly essential to what we do.

Dashi Stock

Makes 1 litre (35fl oz)

7.5g (¼oz) dried shiitake mushrooms
1½ tsp table salt
2 tbsp tamari soy sauce
15g (½oz) kombu (dried kelp)

Dashi is the backbone of so much Japanese cooking – a clean and umami-rich stock. Much of its flavour is derived from kombu (dried kelp), and we also pack this recipe with shiitake mushrooms. It's an obvious choice of stock for us to use because it's a naturally and deeply tasty vegan stock that adds depth to any dish it's added to, without being too pronounced. The recipe will probably leave you with a little more than you need – lucky you! Add a splash of toasted sesame oil, whisk in a little miso, and take a minute for yourself.

Weigh all the ingredients into a saucepan, pour over 950ml (32fl oz) of water and leave to soak for 1 hour.

Put the pan over a gentle heat and slowly bring up to simmering point. Remove from the heat, cool, then chill. Strain out as you need it. The dashi stock will keep, covered in the fridge, for up to 3 days, or frozen for up to 3 months.

Burnt Vegetable Stock

Makes about 750ml (26fl oz)

4 medium carrots (about 250g/9oz), scrubbed
1 large stalk celery (about 30g/1oz)
1 large Spanish onion (about 250g/9oz), or 2 smaller white onions
1 medium leek (about 125g/4½oz)
3 tbsp rapeseed (canola) oil

Burning the veg might sound counterintuitive, but it's all about unlocking deep, smoky, umami-rich flavour. This stock isn't a by-product – it's a foundation. Use it to add complexity to sauces, soups, or grains wherever you want a little extra depth.

Preheat the oven to 240°C/220°C fan/475°F/Gas mark 9. Chop all the vegetables roughly and spread them out over a roasting tray. Drizzle with rapeseed (canola) oil and roast until charred, tossing every so often to ensure even cooking, 20–30 minutes.

Transfer the vegetables to a large saucepan or stockpot with 1.5 litres (52fl oz) of cold water. Bring to the boil, turn down the heat, simmer until reduced by one-quarter, about 30 minutes, then taste. You're looking for a rich, smoky broth. Reduce further if needed.

Strain through a sieve, pressing to extract as much flavour as possible. Leave gently warming if using straight away, or cool and refrigerate for up to 3 days or freeze for up to 3 months.

Brining Liquid

Makes 5.75 litres (6 quarts)

4 tbsp coriander seeds
155g (5½oz) table salt
2 tbsp black peppercorns
1 tsp juniper berries
60g (2¼oz) caster (superfine) sugar

Brining is a game-changer for veg, especially for porous ones like cauliflower that can be bland the deeper you go. The brine infuses seasoning all the way through, adding depth and brightness before you've even started cooking. It's a simple step that makes a big difference.

Toast the coriander seeds in a dry pan until fragrant. Put 5.75 litres (6 quarts) of water in a large saucepan or stockpot over a medium-high heat and add the coriander seeds and all the other ingredients.

Heat, stirring occasionally, until the sugar and salt have dissolved, then leave to cool. If you are not using it straight away, the brining liquid can be kept in the fridge for up to 1 week.

Chilli Crunch

Makes 250g (9oz)

½ tbsp Sichuan peppercorns
1 whole star anise
5 cinnamon sticks
110g (3¾oz) banana shallots (about 2 medium)
35g (1¼oz) peeled cloves of garlic (about 12 cloves)
25g (1oz) red chillies (about 2½ medium)
340ml (11½fl oz) rapeseed (canola) oil
2¼ tbsp chilli flakes
2¼ tbsp aleppo chilli flakes
1 tbsp smoked paprika
1 tbsp plus 2 tsp tamari soy sauce

This is our take on the ultimate flavour bomb – crisp, fiery, and totally addictive. Bubala's chilli crunch is packed with heat, toasted spices, and just the right amount of umami to bring any dish to life. Spoon it over hummus, roasted vegetables, or straight onto bread. You'll want it on everything, and in our restaurants you'll find it on our Smacked Cucumbers dish, here on page 111.

Lightly crush the Sichuan peppercorns in a spice grinder or a mortar and pestle. Put the star anise and cinnamon sticks in a spice bag or a piece of muslin (cheesecloth) and tie with kitchen string to enclose.

Finely slice the shallots, garlic and chillies, keeping each separate. Heat half the rapeseed oil in a pan over a medium heat for around 4 minutes. Test the oil by dropping in a small piece of chilli. If the oil bubbles, it's ready. Add the Sichuan peppercorns and the bag containing the cinnamon sticks and star anise and simmer gently until the oil smells aromatic. It should take around 10 minutes.

Scoop out the whole spices. Discard the cinnamon sticks and star anise and put the Sichuan peppercorns in a bowl, adding the dried spices and set aside.

Fry the shallots, garlic and chillies in separate batches in the fragrant oil until they are golden brown, then scoop them out and set aside on paper towels to cool and crisp up. They will darken in colour.

Remove the oil from the heat and let it cool. Add the reserved Sichuan peppercorns, dried spices and the tamari, then stir through the crispy shallots, garlic and chillies. Add the remaining oil and mix thoroughly.

Transfer to a sterilised glass jar (see page 24) and store, covered in the fridge, for up to 3 months.

Confit Garlic

Makes 500g (1lb 2oz)

3 tbsp fresh thyme leaves
125ml (4fl oz) olive oil
125ml (4fl oz) rapeseed (canola) oil
250g (9oz) garlic (from about 6 heads), cloves peeled
½ tsp flaky sea salt

This simple process of cooking the garlic slowly results in very soft, very sweet cloves, and a highly flavoured oil. Both are used in a number of recipes throughout this book, such as Labneh with Confit Garlic and Za'atar (see page 60) and Onion Squash with Red and Green Zhoug and Kataifi (see page 148), so this is a good one to have in your fridge. It can be used to improve any salad dressing, or as an alternative to raw garlic that gives a sweeter, more rounded flavour.

Put all the ingredients in a saucepan and bring to a simmer. Turn the heat to low and cook gently until the garlic is soft and the tip of a knife passes through with little resistance and the oil is fragrant, about 35 minutes.

Allow to cool, transfer to a sterilised glass jar (see page 24) and store, covered in the fridge, for up to one month.

PRESERVED CITRUSES

The salty, tangy taste of preserved citruses features in many of our recipes, including the lovage pesto to accompany Ful Medames (see page 163), Sweetcorn Pilpelchuma (see page 107) and Gem, Shiso, Hazelnut and Apple Salad (see page 200).

Preserved Limes

Makes 240g (8½oz)

4 unwaxed limes
2 tsp flaky sea salt
200ml (7fl oz) rapeseed (canola) oil

Top and tail the limes, then slice as thinly as possible. Layer the slices in a glass jar or plastic container, sprinkling salt evenly between each layer. Continue until the lime slices and salt are used up, then pour over the oil, making sure the top layer of limes is completely submerged. Cover and keep in the fridge for 2 weeks before use.

The limes will keep covered in the fridge under a thin layer of oil for up to 3 months.

Preserved Lemons

Makes 240g (8½oz)

2 unwaxed lemons
2 tsp flaky sea salt
1 sprig of rosemary, leaves picked
200ml (7fl oz) rapeseed (canola) oil

Top and tail the lemons, then slice very finely. Layer the slices in a glass jar or plastic container, sprinkling salt and rosemary leaves evenly on every layer. Once you've used all the lemon slices and rosemary, pour over the oil, ensuring all the slices are completely submerged. Cover and keep in the fridge for two weeks before use.

The lemons will keep covered in the fridge under a thin layer of oil for up to 3 months.

PICKLES

All our set menus in the restaurants start with a plate of pickles – a great way to get the guests salivating. Down comes an unassuming, small plate of mixed pickles, and they always take people completely by surprise with their variety and flavour, in shape, size, texture and heat. Our pickle plate sets the intention and standard for the meal to come, and we highly recommend starting your meals in the same way!

All of these are quick pickles that can be made and kept for up to a week in the fridge in their pickling liquid, and eaten within a month. They can be eaten as soon as they're made, but they benefit from at least three days of pickling. As long as you don't double-dip your spoon, the brine can be used a second time.

Pickled Shallots

Makes 200g (7oz)

200g (7oz) banana shallots (about 3 medium)
5 tbsp white wine vinegar
75g (2½oz) caster (superfine) sugar
1 tbsp plus 2 tsp sour cherry molasses

Finely slice the shallots to around 5mm (¼in) thick. Set aside. Combine the vinegar, sugar and sour cherry molasses with 5 tablespoons of water in a small saucepan and cook, stirring, until the sugar has dissolved.

Pack the shallots into a sterilised glass jar (see page 24) and pour the hot pickling liquid over to cover. Seal and leave to cool.

Pickled Cucumbers

Makes 250g (9oz)

250g (9oz) Lebanese cucumbers (about 3 medium)
1½ tsp coarse salt
½ banana shallot
125ml (4fl oz) distilled vinegar
125ml (4fl oz) water
80g (2¾oz) sugar
1 tsp mustard seeds
1 clove of garlic

Slice the cucumbers into roughly 1.5cm (⅝in) rounds, put in a colander set over a bowl, sprinkle with the coarse salt and leave to drain for 1 hour. After the hour is up, rinse off all the salt, squeeze out the excess liquid and transfer the cucumbers to a sterilised glass jar (see page 24).

Put all the other ingredients and 125ml (4fl oz) of water in a saucepan over a gentle heat and stir until the sugar has dissolved. Leave to cool, then pour the pickling liquid over the cucumbers and close the jar to seal.

Soy-Pickled Cucumbers

Makes 500g (1lb 2oz)

20g (¾oz) fresh root ginger, peeled
835g (1lb 13½oz) cucumber (2–3 medium cucumbers), unpeeled
210ml (7½fl oz) sherry vinegar
220ml (7¾fl oz) tamari soy sauce
125g (4½oz) caster (superfine) sugar

Slice the ginger into coins approximately 1cm (½in) thick. Finely slice the cucumber. Transfer the ginger and cucumber to a sterilised glass jar or jars (see page 24).

In a pan, bring the vinegar, tamari and sugar to a boil, stirring as needed, until the sugar has dissolved.

Leave to cool, then pour the pickling liquid over the ginger and cucumber and seal.

Roscoff Onion and Barberry Pickle

Makes 500g (1lb 2oz)

4 Roscoff onions (about 400g/14oz in total)
500ml (17fl oz) red wine vinegar
160g (5¾oz) caster (superfine) sugar
25g (1oz) dried barberries
1 tbsp plus 1 tsp pomegranate molasses

Peel and slice the onions into rings 1cm (½in) thick and put in a sterilised glass jar or jars (see page 24).

In a pan, bring the vinegar, sugar, barberries, pomegranate molasses and 500ml (17fl oz) of water to the boil, stirring to combine.

Pour the liquid over the onions while still hot, then set aside for at least 3 hours.

Harissa Cauliflower Pickle

Makes 500g (1lb 2oz)

1 cauliflower (about 500g/1lb 2oz)
7 cloves of garlic
1 litre (35fl oz) distilled vinegar
2 tbsp salt
320g (11¼oz) caster (superfine) sugar
100g (3½oz) rose harissa

Break the cauliflower into small florets and put them and the garlic cloves in a sterilised glass jar or jars (see page 24).

In a pan, bring the vinegar, salt, sugar and 500ml (17fl oz) of water to the boil, stirring as needed, until the salt and sugar dissolve.

Take off the heat and stir through the harissa. Pour the hot liquid over the cauliflower and garlic and seal.

Pickled Celery

Makes about 400g (14oz)

1 medium head of celery
2 cloves of garlic
20g (¾oz) red chillies (about 2½ medium)
5g (⅛oz) pack (or a handful) fresh curry leaves, picked
1 tbsp coriander seeds
6 cardamom pods
500ml (17fl oz) white wine vinegar
1 tbsp table salt
180g (6¼oz) caster (superfine) sugar
2 tsp mustard seeds
1½ tsp ground turmeric
2 tsp black peppercorns

Slice the celery stalks diagonally into about 5cm (½in) pieces. Put the celery, garlic, chillies and curry leaves in a sterilised glass jar or jars (see page 24).

Toast the coriander seeds and cardamom pods in a dry pan until fragrant.

In a separate pan, combine the vinegar, salt and sugar with 540ml (18¾fl oz) of water and bring to a boil, stirring, until the salt and sugar have dissolved. Stir in the mustard seeds, turmeric and peppercorns, then pour the hot liquid over the celery, garlic and curry leaves and seal.

Shiso Daikon Pickle

Makes 500g (1lb 2oz)

500g (1lb 2oz) red daikon (mooli)
scant tbsp coarse sea salt
250ml (9fl oz) rice vinegar
80g (2¾oz) caster (superfine) sugar
4 shiso leaves

Peel and quarter the daikon lengthways, then slice into 1cm (½in) pieces. Put in a colander set over a bowl, sprinkle with the coarse salt and leave to drain for 1 hour.

Meanwhile, bring the vinegar and sugar up to the boil in a pan, stirring as needed until the sugar has dissolved, then leave to cool.

Rinse the excess salt from the daikon, squeeze out the excess juice and put the daikon in a sterilised glass jar (see page 24) with the shiso leaves. Pour over the cooled pickling liquid and seal.

Pickled Romanesco

Makes 550g (1lb 4oz)

⅓ large romanesco cauliflower (about 500g/1lb 2oz)
165ml (5¼fl oz) cider vinegar
50g (1¾oz) caster (superfine) sugar
8g (¼oz) fresh root ginger
1 tbsp lemon juice
1 tsp coriander seeds
1 tsp fennel seeds
zest from ⅓ unwaxed lemon
zest from ⅓ unwaxed grapefruit

Cut the romanesco into small florets and put in a sterilised glass jar or jars (see page 24).

In a pan, bring the vinegar, sugar, ginger, lemon juice, coriander seeds, fennel seeds and 165ml (5½fl oz) of water to the boil, stirring as needed, until the sugar has dissolved.

Remove from the heat and stir in the lemon and grapefruit zests. Leave to cool, then pour over the cauliflower and seal.

GAZOZ

At Bubala, we like our drinks like we like our food: bold, joyful, and just a little unexpected. Our Gazoz – taken from the Turkish word, which means soda or carbonated drink – are a modern take on a nostalgic classic. But at Bubala, these aren't just any soft drinks. Our Gazoz are layered, living things – fermented fruits, herbs, spices, and florals dancing in sparkling water, crafted with the same care and curiosity we give to everything on the menu.

They're refreshing, beautiful, and completely non-alcoholic, though they're not lacking in spirit. Every sip tells a story of the Levant, reimagined through the Bubala lens. Whether you're starting a meal, skipping the booze, or just in the mood for something bright and botanical, a Gazoz is our way of saying: relax, have fun, and let the bubbles do their thing.

Kiwi and Rose Gazoz

Serves 10

For the kiwi syrup
4 medium kiwi fruit (about 250g/9oz), peeled and sliced into 2cm (¾in) rounds
250g (9oz) caster (superfine) sugar

For the rose syrup
250g (9oz) caster (superfine) sugar
15g (½oz) dried rose petals

To serve
ice
sliced fresh kiwi or reserved kiwi fruit
sparkling water
sage sprigs (optional)

Gazoz is our fizzy love letter to Middle Eastern soda culture: playful, floral, and totally refreshing. This version pairs the tart sweetness of kiwi with the soft perfume of rose, lifted by a splash of citrus and bubbles. It's vibrant, unexpected, and a little bit dreamy – like a cocktail without the booze.

For the kiwi syrup, in a large, sterilised (see page 24) airtight jar, layer the kiwi slices with the sugar, ending up with a layer of sugar at the top. Seal and leave to ferment at room temperature for 7–10 days. (If the temperature is cool, you may need the full 10 days.)

After 2 or 3 days, open the jar to release the air. Make sure the kiwi is fully submerged in the sugar at all times. You may need to top up with a little sugar to ensure the fruit is never exposed to the air.

After 7–10 days, all the sugar should have dissolved and formed a syrup. Strain off the syrup and discard the fruit (or reserve to garnish, if using straight away).

For the rose syrup, put the sugar in a pan with 250ml (9fl oz) of water and heat gently. Stir until the sugar dissolves, then let the sugar syrup cool.

Enclose the rose petals in a square of muslin (cheesecloth) and tie with kitchen string. In a sterilised airtight jar, submerge the muslin ball in the sugar syrup and keep at room temperature for 7 days. When the time is up, remove the muslin ball and discard.

Combine the two syrups in a large sterilised jar and store in the fridge. Use within 2 weeks.

For each serving, pour 50ml (3 tablespoons) of the kiwi and rose syrup into a tall glass, add a generous helping of ice, garnish with sliced kiwi and top up with sparkling water. Add a few sprigs of sage if you're feeling flamboyant. Give it a good mix and serve with a straw.

Lemon and Fennel Seed Gazoz

Serves 10

5 unwaxed lemons, sliced into 2cm (¾in) rounds
15g (½oz) fennel seeds (about 2½ tbsp)
250g (9oz) caster (superfine) sugar

To serve
ice
sparkling water
sprigs of shiso or mint
lemon wedges

Sharp, zesty lemon meets the gentle, aniseed warmth of fennel seed in this bright, effervescent gazoz. It's a drink with bite and balance, refreshing but with a subtle spice that lingers. A sparkling nod to tradition, reimagined the Bubala way.

In a large, sterilised (see page 24) airtight jar, layer the lemon slices, alternating with a thick layer of sugar. Continue until you have used up the lemon slices and sugar, finishing with a layer of sugar on top.

Enclose the fennel seeds in a small piece of muslin (cheesecloth) and tie with kitchen string. Place the muslin bag in the jar on top of the sugar and lemons, seal the jar and leave to ferment for 7 days.

After 2 days, take the top off the jar and release the air. Using a long-handled spoon or a knife, mix the sugar and lemon together in the jar, ensuring the lemon is always completely covered in sugar. Repeat this process each day for the fermenting period. You may need to add a little sugar to make sure the lemon is always covered.

After 7 days, remove the muslin bag and the lemon slices and discard. Store the syrup in the fridge and use within 2 weeks.

For each serving, pour 25ml (1½ tablespoons) of the syrup into a tall glass, add a generous serving of ice, then top up with sparkling water. Garnish with shiso or mint sprigs, and a wedge of lemon and serve with a straw.

MEZZE

Labneh with Confit Garlic and Za'atar

Creamy, tangy labneh is made by straining yoghurt to remove the liquid (whey). This process results in a thicker consistency, similar to cream cheese, but with the characteristic tanginess of yoghurt. Pairing with confit garlic and za'atar is a winner and a dish we simply can't take off the menu.

Serves 6–8

800g (1lb 2oz) full-fat Greek yoghurt
½ tsp table salt

To serve
House Za'atar (see page 40)
60g (2¼oz) Confit Garlic cloves (about 16 cloves; see page 47)
2 tbsp garlic oil (see Confit Garlic, page 47)

Line a sieve (sifter) with muslin (cheesecloth) and sit it over a deep bowl, making sure there is plenty of clearance between the bottom of the sieve and the base of the bowl.

Mix the yoghurt well with the salt, then transfer to the sieve and cover with another piece of muslin. Place a weight on top of the yoghurt – a couple of jars or cans will work well. Leave to drain, covered in the fridge for 2 days, until it has a thick consistency.

When it's ready, retrieve the labneh from the fridge and smooth it onto a serving plate (or plates), making a generous well in the middle. Sprinkle with za'atar and spoon confit garlic cloves into the well, finishing with a glug of the confit garlic oil.

Beetroot Borani

This is our take on a vegan borani, enriched with coconut cream instead of the usual yoghurt. It's such an incredible interpretation and hits the Bubala brief with its tang, heat, sweetness and punch. We use salt-baking to really intensify the flavour of the beetroots.

Serves 6–8

325g (11½oz) beetroots (beets) (about 2 very large)
coarse salt
1 tsp coriander seeds
1 tsp fennel seeds
½ small red chilli, deseeded
1 tbsp plus 1 tsp pomegranate molasses, plus extra to serve
30g (1oz) Preserved Lemons (see page 49)
3 small cloves of garlic
juice of ½ lemon
65g (2¼oz) tahini
55g (2oz) coconut cream
sea salt and freshly ground black pepper

To serve
olive oil, for drizzling
small handful of dill fronds
1 tsp nigella seeds

Preheat the oven to 180°C/160°C fan/350°F/Gas mark 4.

Trim the beetroot (beets) and place them on a bed of coarse salt in a roasting tray. Cover the tray with foil, seal well and bake in the oven for around 40 minutes, or until a knife can be inserted into the beetroot with a little give.

While the beetroot is roasting, toast the coriander and fennel seeds in a dry pan until fragrant, then grind in a mortar and pestle or spice grinder.

Once cool enough to handle, peel the beetroots and slice into chunks. Put the beetroot chunks, ground spices and all the other ingredients in a blender and blitz until smooth, around 2 minutes. Check for consistency (it should be smooth) and seasoning, and adjust as needed.

To serve, smooth the borani onto a large plate, drizzle over the olive oil and pomegranate molasses and garnish with the dill fronds and nigella seeds.

Baba Ganoush

Technically this isn't your most authentic baba ganoush, but the smoky aubergines (eggplant) are puréed until smooth and topped with fragrant curry leaf oil, fried curry leaves and toasted pine nuts. This is all in the cooking of the aubergines and, if you have a barbecue, use it so you can smoke and char the aubergines until they are completely black all over. Head chef Victor is to thank for this one!

Serves 6–8

6 medium aubergines (eggplants) (about 1.2kg (2lb 12oz) in total)
135g (4¾oz) tahini
35g (1¼oz) Confit Garlic (about 8 cloves; see page 47)
scant tsp salt
½ clove of garlic
25g (1oz) white miso
sea salt and freshly ground black pepper

For the garnish

1 tbsp pine nuts
2–3 tbsp rapeseed (canola) oil, for frying
4 sprigs of curry leaf (fresh is best but use the equivalent dried if unavailable)
3 tbsp Curry Leaf Oil (see page 36)

On a barbecue or over an open flame on a gas hob (stovetop), using tongs, grill the aubergines (eggplant) hard for 5–10 minutes, or until charred on the outside and totally soft inside. Leave them to cool in a colander in the sink so any excess liquid drains. When cool, peel them and discard the skins.

Transfer the aubergine flesh along with all the other ingredients to a blender and blitz for about 3 minutes, or until extremely smooth. Check the consistency and seasoning, adjusting as needed.

For the garnish, toast the pine nuts in a small dry pan until golden brown. Set aside. Heat the rapeseed (canola) oil in the same pan over a high heat. When hot, shallow fry the curry leaves in the oil until crispy (they should sizzle when they hit the oil). Drain on a plate lined with paper towels.

To serve, smooth the baba ganoush onto a serving platter and pour the curry leaf oil in a puddle in the middle. Garnish with the toasted pine nuts and fried curry leaves.

Whipped Carrot with Pickled Raisins

Pairing carrot with orange and coriander is a classic, so turning the combo into a dip really works. Salt-baking the carrots keeps all of the flavour and removes all the moisture, to make this a real flavour bomb of a dip.

Serves 4–6

4 large carrots (about 320g/11¼oz), unpeeled
coarse salt
12g (¼oz) Confit Garlic (3–4 cloves; see page 47)
2 tsp white miso paste
1½ tsp agave nectar
large pinch of flaky sea salt
3 tbsp plus 2 tsp orange juice
2 tbsp tahini

For the coriander (cilantro) oil

100g (3½oz) fresh coriander (cilantro)
100ml (3½fl oz) rapeseed (canola) oil

For the pickled raisins

50g (1¾oz) golden jumbo raisins
1 tbsp plus 2 tsp white wine vinegar
2½ tsp caster (superfine) sugar
½ tsp aleppo chilli flakes

To serve

1 tsp coriander seeds, toasted in a dry pan
1 tsp pumpkin seeds, toasted in a dry pan
1 tbsp roughly chopped fresh coriander (cilantro) leaves

Preheat the oven to 200°C/180°C fan/400°F/Gas mark 6. Trim and slice the carrots into large chunks, then place in a roasting tray on a layer of coarse salt. Cover the tray with foil and bake for around 45 minutes, or until the tip of a knife passes easily through the chunks.

Let the carrots cool, then peel them fully, removing any gnarly bits. Place in a blender with the remaining ingredients, blitz until smooth, then taste to check the seasoning, adjusting as needed.

For the coriander oil, put some ice in a large bowl and top up with cold water. Roughly chop the coriander, including the stalks. Set a saucepan of water over a high heat and bring to the boil, then add the coriander. Cook for about 20 seconds, until wilted and darkened slightly in colour, then quickly scoop out and transfer to the ice bath (this will preserve the bright colour).

Once cool, remove the coriander from the ice bath, squeeze out as much water as possible, then transfer to a blender. Add the oil and blend for around 2–3 minutes. Transfer to a small pan set over a high heat and rapidly bring to the boil. Remove from the heat and strain through a fine sieve (sifter) lined with muslin (cheesecloth) and discard the pulp. Set aside. This recipe makes more coriander oil than you need. Store the remainder, covered in the fridge, for up to 1 week.

For the pickled raisins, put the raisins in a heatproof jar or bowl. Heat the vinegar in a pan with the sugar, aleppo chilli flakes and 5 teaspoons of water, stirring to dissolve the sugar, then pour the hot liquid over the raisins. Set aside.

When ready to serve, spoon the carrot dip onto a large plate, garnish with the pickled raisins and drizzle with 3 tablespoons of the coriander oil. Crush the toasted coriander and pumpkin seeds and sprinkle over. Garnish with the fresh coriander.

MOTHER HUMMUS

Over the years, having worked at some of the best Middle Eastern restaurants and tested pretty much every single hummus recipe there is, we believe this is the winner. But everyone else feels the same about theirs too. For us, it is about the temperature (cool), texture (completely smooth) and using the best tahini possible.

The bicarb (baking soda) helps break down the natural pectins in the chickpeas (garbanzo beans), resulting in a quicker cook time and softer chickpeas. This recipe can be simply halved for the recipes that follow. It keeps covered in the fridge for up to 3 days.

Serves 6–8 (Makes 520g/1lb 2½oz)

140g (5oz) dried chickpeas (garbanzo beans)
pinch of bicarbonate of soda (baking soda)
2 cloves of garlic
2 tbsp plus 1 tsp lemon juice
½ tsp cumin seeds
scant tsp table salt
55g (2oz) tahini
sea salt and freshly ground black pepper

Soak the chickpeas for at least 6 hours or overnight in a large container, with three times their volume in water. The next day, strain off the water, cover with fresh water (again three times the volume), adding the bicarbonate of soda; see note, above. Bring to the boil, turn the heat down and simmer until the chickpeas are cooked. They should be completely soft with no bite, with most of the chickpea skins coming away from the peas. This should take around 2 hours.

When you drain them, make sure to keep the cooking liquid, or aquafaba. You will need about 110ml (3¾fl oz) aquafaba for this recipe. You should end up with about 280g (10oz) cooked chickpeas.

Put the cooked chickpeas, garlic, lemon juice, cumin seeds, measured aquafaba and salt in a blender and blitz until completely smooth, scraping down the sides of the blender jug a few times. This could take 5–10 minutes.

Add the tahini and blend for a few more minutes, then taste and check for seasoning, adjusting as needed. The hummus should have a pillowy, silky-smooth texture. It can be a little thinner than desired at this stage as it will thicken in the fridge.

Date and Baharat Crunch Hummus

What was meant to be a topping for our festive set menu became a big favourite and stayed for an entire year. It turns out that date and baharat crunch isn't just for Christmas.

The sweet nature of this crunch makes it a great addition to roast root vegetables, or even tossed with some blanched greens to have with rice for a simple dinner.

Serves 3–4

½ portion Mother Hummus (see page 68)
a few sprigs of fresh coriander (cilantro), leaves picked

For the date and baharat crunch
4–5 tbsp rapeseed (canola) oil
1 medium banana shallot, very finely sliced
4 cloves of garlic, very finely sliced
10–15g (¼–½oz) red chilli, deseeded and very finely sliced
45g (1½oz) dates, stones (pits) removed, chopped
2 tbsp baharat spice mix
1 tbsp plus 2 tsp tamari soy sauce
1½ tsp maple syrup
1 heaped tsp aleppo chilli flakes

For the date and baharat crunch, heat the oil in a frying pan (skillet) to 180°C (360°F) when measured on a digital probe thermometer. If you don't have a thermometer to hand, the oil is ready when a piece of shallot added to the hot oil sizzles and rises to the surface.

When the oil is hot, fry the shallot, garlic and chilli separately until golden and crispy, scooping them out and draining each as you go on a plate lined with paper towels. Once all three are fried, return them and all the remaining crunch ingredients to the oil and stir to mix thoroughly. Take off the heat and set aside to cool. The date and baharat crunch makes more than is needed for the recipe. Store the remainder, covered in the fridge, for up to 3 months.

To serve, spoon the hummus onto a plate, top with the date crunch and garnish with the coriander leaves.

Burnt Butter Hummus

This was inspired by my time in Australia. I tried this dish at Thievery restaurant in Sydney, when Julian Cincotta was executive chef. I was blown away by the combo. The rich burnt butter, which, let's be honest, would be good on anything, complemented the hummus unbelievably. I knew that day, whatever Bubala was to become, it would have a Burnt Butter Hummus. See recipe photo on page 69.

Serves 3–4

½ portion Mother Hummus (see page 68); reserve 4 tbsp of the cooked chickpeas (garbanzo beans) for the dressed chickpeas, below
2 tsp toasted pine nuts
a few sprigs of parsley, leaves picked

For the dressed chickpeas
4 tbsp cooked chickpeas (from Mother Hummus, see page 68)
juice of ½ lemon
drizzle of olive oil
a few picked parsley leaves, coarsely chopped

For the burnt butter topping
60g (2¼oz) unsalted butter
pinch of table salt
pinch of paprika

For the dressed chickpeas, dress with the lemon juice, olive oil, and parsley. Mix well and set aside.

For the burnt butter topping, melt the butter in a small saucepan over a medium heat. As it starts to foam, whisk until the milk solids have caramelised and it has started to smell nutty and has a light hazelnut brown colour. Pour off the butter (discard the solids) and season with the salt and paprika.

To serve, spoon the hummus onto a plate and make a well in the middle. Fill the well with the burnt butter, top with the dressed chickpeas and garnish with the pine nuts and parsley leaves.

Hummus with Harissa, Apricot and Jalapeño Oil

Before opening Bubala Soho, we decided that the Chilli Crunch (see page 46) was better suited elsewhere, away from hummus – but we wanted to create something that had similar features, taken to the next level. The apricot harissa crunch has all this and more, and plays on Moroccan tagine flavours.

Serves 3–4

½ portion Mother Hummus (see page 68)
2 tsp chopped fresh coriander (cilantro) leaves

For the apricot crunch
4 tbsp rapeseed (canola) oil
½ shallot, finely sliced
2 small cloves of garlic, finely sliced
1 jalapeño, finely sliced (no need to deseed)
1 tsp coriander seeds
½ tsp caraway seeds
¾ tsp cumin seeds
2 tsp maple syrup
30g (1oz) dried apricots, chopped
2 tsp tamari soy sauce
40g (1½oz) rose harissa

For the apricot crunch, heat the rapeseed oil in a frying pan (skillet) over high heat until it reaches 180°C (360°F) when tested using a digital probe thermometer. If you don't have a thermometer to hand, add a slice of shallot to the hot oil. If it sizzles, it's ready.

Keeping them separate, fry the shallot, garlic and jalapeño until golden brown and crispy, scooping them out and draining each as you go on a plate lined with paper towels. Let them cool and crisp up.

Fry the coriander, caraway and cumin seeds in the same oil until aromatic and fragrant. Let the oil cool, then add all the remaining crunch ingredients and mix well. This recipe makes more apricot crunch than you will need for the recipe. Store the remainder, covered in the fridge, for up to 3 days.

To serve, spoon the hummus onto a plate, top with the apricot crunch and garnish with the coriander.

HUMMUS EXTRA

In the summer of 2024, we cooked at Lost Village Festival in England's Lincolnshire countryside. We aimed to provide a bowl that was delicious and exactly what you want at a festival: comforting, warm and served with bread. The bowl below is what we served. The elements are interchangeable, making it a great way to use up bits and pieces – like some of the extras made from recipes in this book – for a fantastic lunch.

Serves 4

½ portion Mother Hummus (see page 68)
110g (3¾oz) Pickled Cucumbers (see page 50)
4 tbsp dressed chickpeas (garbanzo beans); see Burnt Butter Hummus, page 71
2 soft-boiled eggs (boiled for 6½ minutes, then cooled and peeled)
2 tbsp Tahini Sauce (see page 38)
1 tsp House Za'atar (see page 40)
1 tbsp chopped parsley leaves
extra virgin olive oil, for drizzling
flatbread, to serve (optional)

For the aubergine (eggplant) curry
2 medium aubergines (eggplant) (about 400g/14oz in total)
2 tbsp fine salt
rapeseed (canola) oil, for frying
180g (6¼oz) coarsely chopped tomatoes
small handful of curry leaves
3 cloves of garlic, blended to a paste
7.5g (¼oz) fresh root ginger, blended to a paste
½ tsp black pepper

For the aubergine curry, halve the aubergines, then slice into 2cm (¾in) strips across each half. Put in a colander set over a bowl, sprinkle with the salt and leave to drain for 1 hour.

While the aubergines are salting, heat 1½ tablespoons of rapeseed (canola) oil in a large pan over a medium heat. When hot, add all the other aubergine curry ingredients, except the lime juice and chilli, and cook, stirring, until the mixture becomes dry. This will take about 20 minutes.

When the salted aubergines are ready, pat them dry with paper towels. Heat 2 tablespoons of rapeseed oil in a separate pan, then fry the aubergine slices until golden, about 3–5 minutes on each side. Fold the fried aubergines into the sauce, stir in the lime juice and chilli and mix well.

Meanwhile, for the tomato salad, slice the onion, tomato and cucumber into even pieces, put in a bowl and mix with the herbs. Dress with the lemon juice and salt.

1 tbsp plus 2 tsp confit garlic oil
(see Confit Garlic, page 47)
½ tsp cumin seeds
½ tsp coriander seeds
pinch of ground turmeric
pinch of ground cinnamon
¾ tsp rose harissa
1½ tsp lime juice
½ red chilli, finely chopped

For the tomato salad
½ small red onion
1 medium tomato
¼ large cucumber
1 tsp picked parsley leaves
1 tsp picked mint leaves
1 tsp lemon juice
pinch of salt

To serve, spoon the hummus into a bowl and around it, add the tomato salad, aubergine curry and pickled cucumber (or any of the optional extras to your liking), then finish with the za'atar and herbs. Drizzle a little extra virgin olive oil over the hummus and serve with flatbread, if you like.

Grapefruit Ezme with Tahini and Pomegranate Molasses

'Ezme' (which translates as 'mashed') is a traditional Turkish mezze dish, a finely chopped or blended salad that features a combination of fresh, spicy and tangy. We added tahini sauce for extra creaminess, grapefruit for a fresh, sour note and we finish it with a good glug of pomegranate molasses to really hit home the tang.

Serves 4–6

¾ medium red onion
¼ green chilli (about 15g/½oz)
2 carli peppers (about 50g/1¾oz)
250g (9oz) ripe vine tomatoes
½ grapefruit, scrubbed
½ clove garlic, finely grated (a Microplane is useful here)
zest of ¼ unwaxed lemon
1 tsp olive oil
1 tsp chopped parsley leaves
pinch of salt

For the dressing

¼ tsp ground allspice
¼ tsp cumin seeds
¼ tsp urfa chilli flakes
1 tbsp pomegranate molasses
1 tsp maple syrup
½ tsp table salt
2 tsp lemon juice
4 tbsp plus 1 tsp rapeseed (canola) oil

To serve

90g (3¼oz) Tahini Sauce (see page 38)
1 tbsp pomegranate molasses
pinch of urfa chilli flakes
1 tbsp chopped parsley leaves
1 tsp olive oil

Finely dice the red onion, green chilli and carli peppers, and deseed and chop the tomatoes, adding them all to a bowl as you go. Zest and segment the grapefruit and add to the diced mixture along with the garlic. Add the lemon zest, olive oil and parsley, and season with salt.

For the dressing, combine all the dressing ingredients, except the oil, in a bowl. Slowly whisk in the oil to form a smooth, emulsified dressing, then pour into the ezme mixture and mix well.

To serve, spoon the tahini sauce onto a plate, then spoon the ezme in the centre on top of the tahini sauce. Drizzle with the pomegranate molasses, sprinkle with the chilli flakes and parsley leaves, and drizzle over the olive oil.

Pumpkin Tirshy, with Spiced Olives and Coriander

Tirshy is a flavourful Moroccan dip made with mashed pumpkin or squash (in this case we have used the sweet delica variety), blended with warm spices and olive oil. It's smooth, creamy, and packed with aromatic flavours.

Serves 4

½ delica pumpkin (about 400–450g/14oz–1lb)
1 butternut squash (about 1kg/2lb 4oz)
2 tbsp olive oil
3 tbsp plus 1 tsp pumpkin stock (see method)
10g (¼oz) Confit Garlic cloves (about 3 cloves; see page 47)
5 tsp coriander seeds, coarsely ground in a spice grinder or mortar and pestle
3½ tsp cumin seeds, coarsely ground in a spice grinder or mortar and pestle
20g (¾oz) rose harissa
zest of 1 unwaxed lemon
salt and freshly ground black pepper
1 tbsp chopped fresh coriander (cilantro) leaves, to serve
drizzle of extra virgin olive oil, to serve

For the spiced olives

250g (9oz) olives (a mix of Kalamata and green), stones (pits) removed
½ tsp chilli flakes
¼ tsp dried rose petals, ground to a powder in a spice grinder or mortar and pestle
⅓ tsp coriander seeds
1 tsp Preserved Lemon Purée, (see page 200)
2 tbsp extra virgin olive oil

Preheat the oven to 180°C/160°C fan/350°F/Gas mark 4. Line a baking tray.

Peel, then dice the pumpkin and squash into 5cm (2in) pieces (reserve the seeds), toss with the olive oil and season with salt and pepper. Spread out on the prepared tray, cover with foil and roast for 30 minutes, or until golden and the tip of a knife passes easily through the flesh. Allow to cool a little, then transfer to a blender.

To make the pumpkin stock, put the pumpkin seeds in a pan with 1 litre (35fl oz) of water, bring to the boil, then turn down the heat and simmer for 20 minutes. Strain, discard the seeds and set the liquid aside.

Add the measured pumpkin stock and the remaining ingredients to the blender containing the roasted squash and blend until smooth. Add a little more of the pumpkin stock if needed to get the desired texture and smoothness.

For the spiced olives, finely chop the olives, then mix in a bowl with the remaining ingredients.

To serve, spoon the pumpkin purée onto a dish and top with 3 tablespoons of the spiced olives. Garnish with fresh coriander and a drizzle of extra virgin olive oil.

Muhammara, with Sour Cherry and Walnut

Middle Eastern Muhammara is usually a coarse paste made with peppers and walnuts. We've hand-chopped it here and kept the walnuts whole for added crunch. The addition of sour cherries seemed to make a lot of sense from a flavour perspective, but it also represents a step away from the traditional, which is how we like it!

Serves 4–6

60g (2¼oz) Tahini Sauce (see page 38)
1 tbsp olive oil
1 tbsp sour cherry molasses
1 walnut, to grate
1 sprig of marjoram, leaves picked

For the muhammara
600g (1lb 5oz) red (bell) peppers (about 5 medium)
15g (½oz) dried sour cherries, rehydrated in hot water
5 tsp aleppo chilli flakes
2 tbsp plus 2 tsp sour cherry molasses
30g (1oz) walnuts, toasted in a dry frying pan (skillet) and crushed
1 tsp salt

For the muhammara, using tongs, roast the peppers, either on a barbecue or over an open flame on a gas hob (stovetop), turning, until the skin is blistered all over. Allow them to cool, then peel, discard the seeds, dice and add to a bowl.

Add the rehydrated sour cherries to the bowl with all the other muhammara ingredients. Mix well.

To serve, spoon the tahini sauce over the base of a plate, then spoon the muhammara on top. Drizzle with olive oil and sour cherry molasses. Grate over the walnut (a Microplane is useful here) and sprinkle over the marjoram leaves.

Butter Bean Masabacha with Leek and Urfa Chilli

Masabacha is a variation of hummus featuring whole or partially mashed chickpeas (garbanzo beans) served in a warm, chunky, flavourful sauce. It would typically be made with chickpeas, but we have used butter beans (lima beans) for a richer, creamier texture. This dish is heartier than other styles of hummus, especially with the addition of barbecued leeks.

Start the recipe by soaking the beans the night before.

Serves 4–6

For the masabacha
65g (2¼oz) dried butter beans (lima beans)
pinch of bicarbonate of soda (baking soda)
1½ tbsp lemon juice
45g (1½oz) tahini
15g (½oz) Confit Garlic (about 4 cloves; see page 47)
¼ tsp cumin seeds
¼ tsp salt

For the barbecued leeks and leek oil
1 medium leek (about 80g/2¾oz); use one with plenty of green leaf
rapeseed (canola) oil
1 tbsp (1oz) amba
¼ onion (about 10g/¼oz), diced
½ tsp urfa chilli flakes
½ tsp aleppo chilli flakes
pinch of table salt

For the masabacha, soak the butter beans overnight in plenty of water. The next day, put in a large pan with fresh water to cover generously, add a pinch of bicarbonate of soda (baking soda), bring to the boil, then turn down the heat and simmer until the beans have a nice soft texture. This will take about 90 minutes.

When the beans are cooked, drain, reserving 3–4 tablespoons of the cooking water. Set aside three-quarters of the cooked beans. Put the remaining one-quarter in a blender and add the remaining masabacha ingredients and the reserved cooking water. Blend for a few minutes until completely smooth, then fold in the reserved cooked beans, so there's a mix of smooth and chunky.

If you are cooking on a barbecue, light it now.

For the leeks, trim away most of the green parts and remove the outer layer. Rinse well and set aside to make the leek oil.

Give the white parts of the leeks a good rinse, then grill them on the hot barbecue until blackened; or use tongs to grill them over an open flame on a gas hob (stovetop), turning until blackened all over and cooked all the way through. When they are done, a skewer should insert easily. Leave to cool, then peel away and discard the blackened skins.

To make the leek oil, prepare an ice bath: put a couple of handfuls of ice and cold water in a large bowl. Slice the reserved green parts of the leek, then weigh them. Transfer to a blender. Measure out double the weight of rapeseed (canola) oil and add that to the blender. Blend for 5 minutes, or until smooth, then transfer the mixture to a saucepan and heat until just simmering. Take off the heat straight away and strain through a sieve (sifter) lined with muslin (cheesecloth) into a bowl. Chill in the ice bath (this process will retain the bright colour).

Chop the barbecued leeks into 1cm (½in) pieces, then mix with most of the leek oil and all the other ingredients.

Spoon the masabacha into a bowl and spoon the leek mix to the centre, then drizzle over the reserved leek oil around the edge of the masabacha to serve.

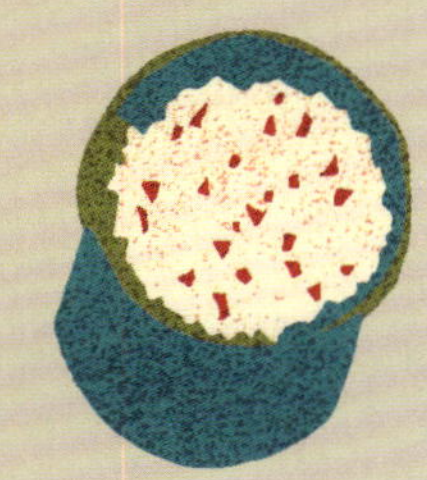

SNACKS

Halloumi with Black Seed Honey

This was a dish that, for all its simplicity, took approximately 16 attempts before we were happy with it. The combination of cheese and honey is a winner but we wanted to take it to the next level. After trying lots of different honeys and spices, and before giving up, we tried black seed honey and the rest is history.

The honey recipe here will make enough for roughly 2 halloumi blocks – perfect for a larger serving size if you want to double the recipe, and it's also delicious with a cheeseboard. See overleaf for recipe photo.

Serves 2–3

225–250g (8–9oz) block halloumi
1 tsp lemon juice and zest of
  1 unwaxed lemon
flaky sea salt

For the black seed honey
1¾ tsp coriander seeds
2½ tsp nigella seeds
4 tsp whole black peppercorns
½ tsp urfa chilli flakes
125g (4½oz) clear blossom honey

Preheat the oven to 180°C/160°C fan/350°F/Gas mark 4.

For the black seed honey, toast the coriander seeds in a dry frying pan (skillet) until fragrant and just changing colour, then transfer to a pestle and mortar with the nigella seeds, peppercorns and chilli flakes and roughly grind. Combine with the honey. Set aside. The recipe makes more than you need, so keep the remainder in a sealed jar in the fridge for up to 3 months.

Heat a frying pan (skillet) over a medium heat, add the halloumi and fry on all sides until turning golden. Transfer to a baking tray and heat in the oven for 15 minutes.

Drizzle with the lemon juice and generously spoon over the black seed honey (about 3 tablespoons is perfect). Sprinkle over a little lemon zest and a pinch of sea salt to serve.

Halloumi with Chamomile and Fennel Honey

We wanted a new take on our original halloumi dish and found that the chamomile added a really great floral note that complemented both the honey and the cheese – we have chef Jake Norman to thank for this. You should be able to get hold of the dried flowers from health-food stores. The honey will store for 3 months and can be used as an alternative to your regular honey. See overleaf for recipe photo.

Serves 2–3

225–250g (8–9oz) block halloumi
1 tsp lemon juice and zest of 1 unwaxed lemon
flaky sea salt

For the chamomile and fennel honey (Makes 250g/9oz)
2 tsp fennel seeds
scant tsp cumin seeds
8 tbsp dried chamomile flowers
215g (7½oz) clear honey
2 tbsp plus 2 tsp olive oil
1 tbsp aleppo chilli flakes

Preheat the oven to 180°C/160°C fan/350°F/Gas mark 4.

For the chamomile and fennel honey, toast the fennel and cumin seeds in a dry pan until fragrant. Transfer to a food processor, add the dried chamomile flowers and lightly blend so that the flowers retain their shape (don't blend to a powder).

Transfer to a saucepan, add the honey and the remaining ingredients and heat gently, using a whisk to mix well. Set aside. The recipe makes more than you need, so keep the remaining chamomile and fennel honey in a sealed jar in the fridge for up to 3 months.

Fry the halloumi in a hot frying pan (skillet) until golden on each side. Transfer to a baking tray and heat in the oven for 15 minutes.

Drizzle with the lemon juice and add 2–3 tablespoons of the chamomile and fennel honey. Sprinkle over the lemon zest and finish with a pinch of sea salt to serve.

Falafel with Tahini Sauce, Sumac Onions and Amba Sauce

This is a real Bubala classic that's been on since day one and will never leave! Our falafel are herbier than most, which gives them an amazing bright green centre when you break them open. This recipe makes enough falafel balls to serve about 8 people with other dishes alongside (we serve 3 pieces for 2 people to share in the restaurant).

You will need to get the chickpeas (garbanzo beans) soaking the night before making this recipe.

Makes 25 falafel balls (Serves 8)

For the falafel spice mix

50g (1¾oz) cumin seeds
50g (1¾oz) coriander seeds
40g (1½oz) ground cardamom seeds
15g (½oz) ground cinnamon

For the sumac onions (Makes about 100g/3½oz)

1 red onion (about 100g/3½oz)
pinch of flaky sea salt
1 tsp lemon juice
¾ tsp sumac

For the falafel balls

1 large white onion (about 150g/5½oz), roughly chopped
4 cloves of garlic, roughly chopped
2 red chillies, roughly chopped
45g (1½oz) parsley, leaves picked
115g (4oz) fresh coriander (cilantro), leaves picked
200g (7oz) dried chickpeas (garbanzo beans), soaked overnight (to give 400g/14oz soaked)
20g (¾oz) falafel spice mix (from recipe above)
2 tsp baking powder
1 heaped tsp table salt
rapeseed (canola) oil, for frying

For the falafel spice mix, toast the cumin and coriander seeds in a dry pan until fragrant. Grind to a powder in a pestle and mortar or spice grinder and combine with the remaining spice mix ingredients. This recipe makes more spice blend than you need here, so keep the remainder in a sealed jar in your spice cupboard.

For the sumac onions, finely slice the onion and transfer to a glass or ceramic bowl. Toss with the salt and lemon juice, leave to marinate for 1 hour, then add the sumac and mix well. Set aside.

For the falafel balls, blend the onion, garlic and chillies in a blender to a fine paste. Push the paste through a fine sieve (sifter) or squeeze in a clean piece of muslin (cheesecloth) to remove as much moisture as possible. Set aside.

Working in small batches, pulse the herbs and chickpeas in a food processor to form a coarse mix. Transfer to a bowl and fold in the onion mixture, the falafel spice mix, the baking powder and the salt. Use your hands to shape the falafel mixture into about 25 even-sized balls.

Next, fry the falafel. To deep fry, fill a large, heavy-based pan with oil to a depth of about 8cm (3½in), ensuring there is plenty of free space to allow for the oil to expand during heating. Heat the oil to 180°C (360°F), which will take around 15 minutes.

Recipe continued overleaf...

To serve
50–75g (1¾–2½oz) Tahini Sauce (see page 38)
40g (1½oz) amba (see page 34), let down with 2 tsp water
large pinch of House Za'atar (see page 40)

Test with a digital probe thermometer. If you don't have a probe to hand, test the oil temperature by dropping in a small amount of falafel mix; it should bubble vigorously but not be smoking. When the oil is ready, fry the falafels until they float to the surface and are golden brown all over, about 5 minutes. Fry in batches if needed.

If you prefer to shallow fry, the same timings apply. Just heat 2–3cm (¾–1¼in) oil in a large, heavy-based pan.

Remove the cooked falafels with a slotted spoon and drain on a plate lined with paper towels while you cook the rest. Keep warm.

To serve, spoon the tahini sauce onto a plate, add the amba sauce to one side and the falafel balls in the middle. Garnish with the sumac onions and a pinch of za'atar

Friggitelli Peppers with Black Garlic Tahini and Sesame Crumb

For Bubala's fifth birthday, we hosted a series of dinners in collaboration with friends of the restaurant. This dish came about from a collaboration with chef Lewis de Haas, from London restaurant Crispin. It pulls together elements used in other dishes to season the delicious friggitelli pepper – the bittersweet, Italian cousin to the Spanish padrón. You could also cook these peppers on a hot barbecue, for added char.

Serves 4

3 tbsp vegetable oil
16–20 friggitelli peppers
60g (2¼oz) Black Garlic Tahini (see page 39)
40g (1½oz) Sesame Crumb (see page 43)

Heat the oil in a frying pan (skillet) over a high heat. When hot, fry the peppers, turning, until they blister and start to take on colour. Remove from the heat.

To serve, spread the black garlic tahini on a serving plate, pile the peppers up high and dress generously with the sesame crumb,

Petit Violet Artichokes, with Sichuan Salt and Blood Orange Aioli

Carciofi alla giudia is a traditional recipe from Roman Jewish cuisine. It's usually made with a large mammole artichoke, but we have used the smaller petit violet variety here to make the dish easier to share. The Sichuan salt is far from traditional, but it adds a tingling and numbing sensation – very moreish when you dip into the blood orange aioli. Eat these with your hands!

Serves 4

8 petit violet artichokes
rapeseed (canola) oil, for confiting and frying
blood orange wedges, to serve

For the Sichuan salt
2 tsp Sichuan peppercorns
4 tbsp flaky sea salt

For the blood orange aioli
50g (1¾oz) blood orange peel (from 1–2 oranges)
3 tbsp plus 1 tsp blood orange juice
3 tbsp soy milk
10g (¼oz) miso paste
1 tsp tamari soy sauce
½ tsp sugar
1 tsp toasted sesame oil
2 tsp moscatel vinegar
1 tsp salt
100ml (3½fl oz) rapeseed oil

For the Sichuan salt, toast the peppercorns in a hot dry pan until they are fragrant, being careful not to let them burn. Blitz to a coarse powder in a spice grinder and mix through the salt. Set aside. This recipe makes more Sichuan salt than you need, so store the remainder in a sealed jar in your spice cupboard.

For the blood orange aioli, blanch the blood orange peel three times in boiling water, scooping the peels out and changing the water each time, then put in a blender with all the other aioli ingredients except the rapeseed oil and blend until smooth. Slowly drizzle in the oil and blend for about 10 seconds to form a smooth, thick, emulsified sauce. Set aside.

Peel off and discard the tough outer leaves of the artichokes (about two layers), until the more delicate, pale leaves are revealed. Trim away the tough stalks to around 6cm (2½in), or to where a knife can cut through them easily. Use a sharp peeler to peel away the stalk and base of the artichoke, revealing the white heart. Cut off the tops of the tougher leaves.

Next, confit the artichokes. Pour enough rapeseed oil in a deep, heavy-based pan to fully submerge the artichokes and heat to 120°C (250°F). A digital probe thermometer is useful here but if you don't have one, the oil is ready for confiting when there is a slight sizzle when the artichokes go into the oil.

Recipe continued overleaf...

Add the artichokes and cook over a gentle heat for 10–15 minutes, or until a knife can be easily inserted into the thickest part of the base with little resistance. Remove the artichokes with a slotted spoon and set aside.

To finish, deep fry the confit artichokes using the same pan and oil. Heat the oil to 180°C (360°F). the oil is ready when a small piece of artichoke sizzles when it goes into the hot oil. Add the artichokes and fry for 2–3 minutes, or until the outer leaves start to open up like a blooming flower, and to crisp up. Remove with a slotted spoon, drain on a plate lined with paper towels, then season lightly with the Sichuan salt.

To serve, place the artichokes off-centre of a large serving plate. Garnish with blood orange wedges and serve with a dipping bowl of blood orange aioli and additional Sichuan salt.

Sprouts with Dates and Harissa Crumb

This take on the festive favourite will ensure you never boil a sprout again. The whipped tofu here is based on a classic French vinaigrette and should be quite loose in texture. It carries a real mustard punch, and any leftovers you're lucky enough to end up with will liven up your salads!

Serves 4

30–35g (1–1¼oz) medjool dates, stones (pits) removed
olive oil, for drizzling
130g (4½oz) Brussels sprouts
rapeseed (canola) oil, for frying
2 tbsp capers, drained
2 tsp lemon juice
10 sprigs of dill

For the harissa crumb
2½ tsp rapeseed oil
20g (¾oz) panko breadcrumbs
15g (½oz) rose harissa
sea salt and freshly ground black pepper

For the mustard-whipped tofu
290g (10¼oz) pack tofu, drained
85g (3oz) Dijon mustard
2 cloves of garlic
20g (¾oz) piece of white onion
5 tbsp sherry vinegar
1½ tsp salt
1½ tsp cracked black pepper
2 tbsp olive oil
zest of ¼ unwaxed lemon

For the harissa crumb, heat 2½ teaspoons of rapeseed oil in a frying pan (skillet), add the breadcrumbs and toast until golden brown. Towards the end of the toasting time, stir in the harissa. Season with salt and pepper and set aside to cool.

For the mustard-whipped tofu, put all the ingredients and 6 tablespoons of water in a blender and blend until smooth. Taste for seasoning. It should be punchy. This recipe makes more mustard-whipped tofu than you will need for this recipe. Store the remainder in the fridge for up to 3 days.

Chop the dates in half, and each half into thirds. Dress with a little olive oil to prevent sticking and set aside.

Bring a small pan of salted water to the boil. Halve the sprouts and blanch them for 45 seconds to 1 minute, then scoop out and refresh in a bowl of ice-cold water. Squeeze the capers to remove as much brine as possible and pat dry.

Heat 5cm (2in) of rapeseed oil in a heavy-based pan until it reaches 180°C (360°F) on a digital probe thermometer. If you don't have a thermometer to hand, it is ready when a sprout dropped into the hot oil sizzles. It should take about 5 minutes to reach temperature. Working in batches if needed (don't overcrowd the pan), drop the sprouts into the hot oil and deep fry, turning, until deep golden brown. Remove the sprouts with a slotted spoon and drain on paper towels,

Recipe continued overleaf...

Briefly fry the capers in the hot oil until they stop sizzling and turn crispy, then scoop out and drain on a plate lined with paper towels.

Toss the fried sprouts with the lemon juice, 2 tablespoons of the harissa crumb, the crispy capers, the dill sprigs and the chopped dates.

To serve, spoon about 4–5 tablespoons of the whipped tofu onto a large serving plate and spread it over the base. Pile the sprouts on top and sprinkle more harissa crumb over to finish.

Aubergine with Zhoug and Date Syrup

This dish was on the menu at the first pop-up that Helen and I did together. It was a dish Helen had created before and it worked perfectly, with the spicy zhoug, fried oily aubergines and the sweetness of the date syrup. It's a perfect starter when having friends over as it's simple and it's all in the prep! The leftover zhoug is perfect in a sandwich or on top of your hummus for a spicy kick.

Serves 4

2 medium aubergines (eggplants) (about 400g/14oz in total)
4 tbsp rapeseed (canola) oil
4 tsp date syrup
pinch of flaky sea salt

For the zhoug (Makes about 250g/9oz)
1 small clove of garlic
½ red chilli, deseeded
100g (3½oz) fresh coriander (cilantro), leaves picked
100ml (3½fl oz) rapeseed oil
2 tsp Hawaij Spice Blend (see page 42)
pinch of chilli flakes
1 tbsp plus 2 tsp lemon juice
large pinch of flaky sea salt

For the zhoug, pulse the garlic and chilli in a blender until finely chopped. Add half the coriander leaves and half the oil, then blend until smooth. Add the remaining coriander, remaining oil, the spices and lemon juice, and blend again until completely smooth. Season to taste with flaky sea salt. Set aside. This recipe makes more zhoug than you need, so store the remainder in a sealed jar in the fridge for up to 3 days.

Slice the aubergines into 2cm (¾in) rounds. Heat the oil in a large frying pan (skillet) over a medium heat. When hot, working in batches, add the aubergine slices and fry until golden, for at least 5 minutes on each side.

Remove the slices using a slotted spoon and drain on a plate lined with paper towels. Keep warm while you cook the rest.

Serve the aubergine slices on a large serving platter, topped with the zhoug, with the date syrup drizzled over. Scatter with flaky sea salt.

Lemon Pepper Fried Cauliflower

For this recipe, you'll need to steam and flour the cauliflower at least 2 hours ahead – ideally the day before. Keep the florets covered in the fridge for as long as possible, to really maximise the crispiness.

The spice blend here makes this dish. Full of zingy black lime and dried lemon, the coating will leave you wanting more. You can toss all sorts of fried vegetables in it and they are sure to be banging!

Serves 4

1 small cauliflower (about 400g/14oz), trimmed
rapeseed (canola) oil, for deep frying
small bunch of parsley, leaves picked, to serve
2 spring onions (scallions), finely chopped, to serve

For the cauliflower flour mix

50g (1¾oz) potato starch
50g (1¾oz) rice flour

For the cauliflower spice mix

1 tbsp cumin seeds
½ tbsp coriander seeds
20g (¾oz) dehydrated lemon or zest of 1 unwaxed lemon
10g (¼oz) dried black lime
2 tbsp plus 1 tsp soft dark brown sugar
1 tbsp table salt
¾ tsp black peppercorns
½ tbsp whole white peppercorns

Chop the cauliflower into small, bite-size florets. Bring a pan of water to the boil, add the cauliflower florets and boil for 3–4 minutes. Drain well, then transfer to a bowl and cool.

For the flour mixture, combine the potato starch and rice flour. Once the cauliflower is cool, add the flour mixture and mix until the florets are well coated. Set aside for a minimum of 2 hours, or cover and refrigerate overnight for maximum crispiness.

Meanwhile, for the spice mix, toast the cumin and coriander seeds in a dry pan until fragrant. In a spice grinder, grind the dehydrated lemon and black lime to make a fine powder, then add the toasted seeds and all the remaining spice mix ingredients and blend until finely ground. Set aside.

For the velvet tomatoes, put all the ingredients except the oil in a blender and blend for 10 minutes, until very smooth. Slowly add the oil, blending between additions, then blend for another 5 minutes, until it has a semi-thick, smooth and velvety consistency. Taste and check the seasoning. Set aside.

For the lemon maple syrup, mix the two ingredients together in a bowl until incorporated.

Recipe continued overleaf...

For the velvet tomatoes

150g (5½oz) vine tomatoes (2–3 medium), quartered, seeds removed
1 clove of garlic
½ red chilli
scant tsp cumin seeds
½ tsp agave nectar
½ tsp table salt
5 tbsp plus 1 tsp rapeseed oil

For the lemon maple syrup

1 tbsp lemon juice
1 tsp maple syrup

Heat about 8cm (3¼in) rapeseed oil in a heavy-based saucepan on a medium heat until it reaches 180°C (360°F). You can test this with a digital probe thermometer if you have one. If not, drop a piece of cauliflower into the hot oil. If it sizzles, you're good to go. If not, wait a bit longer.

When it's ready, working in batches, fry the cauliflower for 2–3 minutes, or until crispy and golden. Remove with a slotted spoon, drain on a plate lined with paper towels and keep warm while you fry the rest.

Toss the cauliflower with 2 spoonfuls of the spice mix. This recipe makes more spice mix than you need, so store the remainder in a sealed jar.

To serve, spoon the velvet tomatoes into a bowl and top with the cauliflower. Drizzle over the lemon maple syrup and garnish with the parsley and spring onions to serve.

Sweetcorn Pilpelchuma

Pilpelchuma is a traditional Libyan chilli-garlic paste. We added further flavour with the addition of black garlic, sesame seeds and preserved lemon. Spread on just about anything.

Serves 6–8

2 cobs of sweetcorn (ears of corn), peeled and trimmed, quartered (to give 8 pieces in total)
20g (¾oz) Pickled Shallots (see page 50)
small chunk of ricotta salata, to serve

For the pilpelchuma butter
80g (2¾oz) sesame seeds
100g (3½oz) butter
1½ tsp cumin seeds
1 tsp caraway seeds
1 tsp aleppo chilli flakes
2 tsp smoked paprika
1 tsp ground cinnamon
1 tsp lemon juice
20g (¾oz) Preserved Lemons (see page 49)
1 dried cascabel chilli, soaked in boiling water, stems and seeds removed
1½ tsp black garlic
5 cloves Confit Garlic (see page 47)
1 tsp flaky sea salt

For the pilpelchuma butter, preheat the oven to 180°C/160°C fan/350°F/Gas mark 4 and line four small baking trays with baking paper. Put the sesame seeds on one lined tray, then toast in the oven until golden, 5–10 minutes. Set aside. Keep the oven on for the pumpkin seed crumble.

Melt the butter in a pan on a medium heat and cook, stirring, until the butter foams, then turns a nut-brown colour and smells toasty (don't let it burn). Take off the heat, then add all the other dried seeds and spices.

Set aside to cool. Just before the butter has set, put all the remaining butter ingredients in a blender and pulse to mix. Add the browned butter mixture and blend until smooth and emulsified. Finally, fold in the sesame seeds. Set aside.

For the pumpkin seed crumble, keeping them separate, lightly dress the pumpkin seeds and both types of sesame seeds with the vegetable oil. Transfer to the three remaining lined trays and toast to a dark golden colour. This will take 5–15 minutes. They may darken at different speeds so keep a close eye – the sesame seeds will turn the quickest.

Recipe continued overleaf...

For the pumpkin seed crumble
40g (1½oz) pumpkin seeds
2 tsp white sesame seeds
2 tsp black sesame seeds
2 tsp smoked paprika
1½ tbsp vegetable oil
pinch of flaky sea salt

Transfer the seeds to a plate lined with paper towels to remove the excess oil, then put in a blender with the smoked paprika and flaky sea salt and blitz to form a coarse rubble. This recipe makes more pumpkin seed crumble than you will need for this recipe, so keep the remainder in a sealed jar.

Bring a large pan of seasoned water to the boil and cook the sweetcorn for 10 minutes, then turn off the heat and leave in the water.

To finish the sweetcorn, heat the barbecue. When hot, grill the pieces of corn, turning, until just charred, then toss in 2–3 tablespoons of the butter. (You could also cook this inside, under the grill/broiler). To serve, spread 2 tablespoons of the butter on a plate, top with the corn and spoon more butter on top. Pile on the pickled shallots and sprinkle over the pumpkin seed crunch. To finish, grate over a little ricotta salata.

Smacked Cucumbers

This is our take on a Chinese classic – it's a real winner and perfect for so many occasions. Our twist includes the addition of maple tahini and preserved lime, and the result is a dish that, once tasted, will never be forgotten. Use the smaller Lebanese cucumbers if you can get your hands on them, as they are a little sweeter and crisper.

Serves 4

600g (1lb 5oz) cucumbers (about 2 medium)
coarse salt
150g (5½oz) Chilli Crunch (see page 46)

For the maple tahini

4 tsp lime juice
10g (¼oz) fresh root ginger
3 tbsp tamari soy sauce
90g (3¼oz) tahini
3 tbsp maple syrup

For the dressing

1½ tsp toasted sesame oil
½ tsp tamari soy sauce
large pinch of flaky sea salt
2 tsp agave nectar
2 tsp lime juice
4 tsp olive oil

Top and tail the cucumbers (keep the skin on), put them on a sturdy chopping board and, using a small saucepan or frying pan, smack them hard enough several times to break the skin in several places. Slice down the middle lengthways and chop into roughly 2cm (¾in) rounds.

Transfer to a colander set over a bowl, season generously with coarse salt and leave to drain for 1 hour.

Meanwhile, for the maple tahini, blend the lime juice and ginger together in a mortar and pestle or a mini food processor, then pass through a fine sieve (sifter). Discard the solids.

Transfer to a bowl, add all the remaining maple tahini ingredients, mix well and taste to check the seasoning. Set aside.

For the dressing, combine all the ingredients except the oil in a bowl using a hand whisk, then slowly whisk in the oil to form a smooth, emulsified dressing. Set aside.

When the hour is up, rinse the salt from the cucumbers, pat dry, then dress with the dressing. Spoon all of the maple tahini into a bowl, pile with the dressed cucumbers and sprinkle over the chilli crunch liberally to serve.

Fritto Misto

We thought it would be fun to add a fritto misto-style dish to our menu, but we wanted to include a little surprise. The orange, with the skin left on, can be eaten whole, and the olives are borderline addictive. The dressing adds a nice bit of sweetness, balanced with some spice.

Serves 6

2 heads of fennel
rapeseed (canola) oil, for deep frying
6 slices of orange, scrubbed, left unpeeled
6 pitted gordal olives
flaky sea salt

For the frying flour
100g (3½oz) rice flour
100g (3½oz) potato flour (potato starch)
50g (1¾oz) polenta

For the orange dressing
5 tbsp orange juice
1 tsp fennel seeds
1 tsp merlot vinegar
½ tsp aleppo chilli flakes
½ tsp agave nectar

For the fennel blanching liquid
3 tbsp plus 1 tsp salt
4 tbsp white wine vinegar
2 tbsp sugar

For the frying flour, mix all the ingredients in a bowl, making sure there are no lumps. Set aside.

For the orange dressing, bring the orange juice to the boil in a small pan and reduce by two-thirds. Toast the fennel seeds in a dry pan until fragrant, then transfer to a mortar and pestle and crush. Combine the orange juice, fennel seeds and the remaining dressing ingredients in a bowl, whisking well. Set aside

Remove and discard the tough outer leaves of the fennel, leaving a fist-sized core, then cut into 30g (1oz) wedges through the core (to hold the wedges together). Reserve the fronds.

For the fennel blanching liquid, bring 1.6 litres (54fl oz) of water to the boil in a large saucepan, adding the salt, vinegar and sugar. Blanch the fennel wedges for 1 minute, then scoop out and refresh in a bowl of iced water. Pat dry and set aside.

Heat 5cm (2in) of rapeseed oil in a heavy-based pan until it reaches 180°C (360°F) on a digital probe thermometer. If you don't have a thermometer, drop a small piece of fennel into the hot oil. If it sizzles, you're good to go. If not, wait a bit longer. When the oil is ready, coat the fennel wedges, orange slices and olives in the frying flour, shaking off any excess. Working in batches, deep fry until golden and crispy, then scoop out using a slotted spoon, drain on a plate lined with paper towels and lightly season with flaky sea salt. Keep warm while you fry the rest.

Serve on a plate, finishing with a sprinkle of the chopped fennel fronds, with the dressing on the side.

Persimmon with Chestnut and Miso

There are a few varieties of persimmon available. We use fuyu or sharon, which can be eaten while still firm. These varieties are available during the winter months and add a much-needed splash of colour and freshness to the menu. Here, they are served with chestnuts, a classic pairing from northern Italy. The addition of wakame, despite seeming a left-field addition, gives a salinity to the dish, which nicely complements the sweetness of the persimmons.

Serves 6

For the pickled persimmon and wakame

450g (1lb) persimmons (about 3)
2 tbsp dried wakame seaweed
2 dried black limes, crushed in a mortar and pestle
2 tsp cracked black pepper
1 tbsp mustard seeds
2 tsp coriander seeds
5 cloves of garlic (about 15g/½oz, peeled weight)
2 cardamom pods, crushed
1 clove, crushed
240ml (8fl oz) white wine vinegar
120g (4¼oz) sugar
½ tsp salt
135g (4¾oz) red chicory (endive), sliced, to serve

For the chestnut miso

100g (3½oz) cooked, peeled chestnuts
35g (1¼oz) white miso
1 tsp agave nectar
1 tsp sherry vinegar
½ clove of garlic
pinch of salt

For the chestnut crumb

100g (3½oz) cooked, peeled chestnuts
35g (1¼oz) sesame seeds
85g (3oz) soft dark brown sugar
pinch of flaky sea salt

Preheat the oven to 150°C/130°Cfan/300°F/Gas mark 2.

For the pickled persimmons, slice the persimmons in half horizontally, then cut each half into quarters, so you get 8 pieces from each. Put the pieces in a large heatproof bowl.

Put the wakame in a separate, small heatproof bowl.

Put all the remaining pickling ingredients in a pan with 240ml (8fl oz) of water and bring to the boil. Pour the hot liquid over the sliced persimmons and the wakame, then set both aside and allow to cool. When cool, drain and set aside.

Meanwhile, for the chestnut miso, put all the ingredients in a blender with 100ml (3½fl oz) of water and blend until smooth.

For the chestnut crumb, pulse the chestnuts in a blender to form a coarse crumb. Don't overmix. Spread out evenly in a single layer on a baking sheet and bake in the hot oven until they are completely dried out and beginning to turn darker. This should take about 30 minutes in total. Toss halfway to make sure they are colouring evenly. When they are ready, set aside and leave them to cool.

Toast the sesame seeds in a dry pan until golden. Transfer to a blender, adding the dried chestnuts and the sugar and salt. Pulse just enough to break up the sesame seeds, but not so the mixture becomes a powder.

To serve, spoon the chestnut miso onto a large serving plate and spread it around in a circle. Combine the pickled persimmons, wakame and chicory in a bowl. Lay them over the top of the miso and spoon over the chestnut crumb.

SKEWERS

Oyster Mushroom Skewers

Arguably, our most popular dish! These skewers can convert any mushroom hater. In the early days at Bubala, we would offer people their money back if they tried them and didn't like them. There is nothing not to like: great texture, full of umami, sticky, sweet, and often compared to a meat counterpart. Other types of mushrooms do work but oyster mushrooms soak up a lot of the flavour and we think these work best. If you can, give the mushroom some flames on the barbecue; it makes all the difference.

Serves 6

600g (1lb 5oz) oyster mushrooms

For the mushroom marinade
2 cloves of garlic
135ml (4½fl oz) tamari soy sauce
2 tbsp plus 1 tsp agave nectar
4 tsp coriander seeds
120ml (3¾fl oz) rapeseed (canola) oil

6 metal or wooden skewers (if using wooden, soak them in water for 30 minutes before use to prevent burning)

For the marinade, put the garlic and 1 tablespoon of the tamari in a blender or mini food processor and blend to form a smooth paste. Add the agave nectar, coriander seeds and remaining tamari and blend. Once thoroughly combined, slowly add the oil, blending between additions, to form a smooth, emulsified sauce.

Break or tear the mushrooms into (5cm) 2in pieces. Transfer to a lipped baking tray and brush with two-thirds of the marinade. Cover and leave to marinate overnight in the fridge.

The next day, thread 100g (3½oz) of the marinated mushrooms onto each of 6 metal skewers. Light the barbecue.

While the barbecue is heating, strain off the excess oil from the remaining marinade. Put it in a small saucepan set over a low heat and reduce the marinade until it is thick.

When the barbecue is hot, slowly cook the skewers, turning regularly until they are nicely caramelised. Drizzle the cooked skewers with the reduced marinade and serve.

Note
For all of the skewer recipes here, you will need to start the day before to give time for overnight marination. Cooking on a barbecue will give the best results but they can also be cooked indoors under a hot grill (broiler).

15cm (6in) metal skewers are ideal, but you can use bamboo ones – just make sure you soak them before use.

Leek Skewers with Amba

This is a little play on the magic combo of leeks and mustard. Amba is a spicy, pickled sauce made with green mangoes, mustard seeds, turmeric, fenugreek, chilli powder, vinegar and salt. It's tangy, slightly spicy and has a hint of sweetness. It provides such a great marinade for the leeks, which gives them a sweet, sour and spicy finish once charred on the barbecue.

Serves 6

600g (1lb 5oz) leeks, green tops trimmed away (about 6 medium, trimmed weight)
½ lemon

For the amba marinade
½ dried black lime
3 tbsp agave nectar
1 tbsp plus 2 tsp lemon juice
½ tsp table salt
50g (1¾oz) amba (see page 34)
5 tbsp plus 1 tsp rapeseed (canola) oil

6 metal or wooden skewers (if using wooden, soak them in water for 30 minutes before use to prevent burning)

For the marinade, put the dried black lime in a blender or mini food processor and blend to a powder. Add all the remaining marinade ingredients except the oil, and blend. Once thoroughly combined, slowly add the oil, blending between additions to form a smooth, emulsified sauce.

Chop the leeks into 4cm (1½in) discs and rinse well. Transfer to a steamer and steam them for 5–8 minutes, or until they are soft. Set aside to cool, then arrange the leeks on a lipped baking tray and pour 150ml (5fl oz) of the marinade over them. Marinate overnight, or for at least 3 hours, covered, in the fridge.

Meanwhile, in a small pan over a low heat, slowly reduce the remaining marinade to a thick sauce. Set aside.

When the leeks have marinated, thread 100g (3½oz) of leek discs onto each of 6 metal skewers. Light the barbecue. When hot, cook the leek skewers, making sure to caramelise them evenly, turning where necessary. This should take 5–10 minutes. Transfer to a serving plate, adding a squeeze of lemon juice and a drizzle of the reduced marinade.

Napa Cabbage Skewers with Preserved Lime and Cardamom

Cabbages are so good cooked on the barbecue. Using Napa cabbage (also called Chinese cabbage) has a great ratio between leaf and stalk, which works perfectly as a skewer.

Serves 6

600g (1lb 5oz) Napa cabbage

For the marinade

75g (2½oz) Preserved Limes (see page 49)
7 cloves of garlic (about 20g/¾oz), peeled weight)
3 tbsp plus 2 tsp maple syrup
1 tbsp lemon juice
1 tsp freshly ground cardamom seeds
1½ tsp table salt
150ml (5fl oz) rapeseed (canola) oil

6 metal or wooden skewers (if using wooden, soak them in water for 30 minutes before use to prevent burning)

For the marinade, put all the marinade ingredients, except the oil, in a blender or mini food processor and blend to a smooth paste. Once thoroughly combined, slowly add the oil, blending between additions, to form a smooth, emulsified sauce.

Cut the cabbage into quarters lengthways, remove the core, then cut into 5cm (2in) pieces. Arrange the pieces on a lipped baking tray and pour over two-thirds of the marinade. Leave to marinate, covered in the fridge, for at least 3 hours or overnight.

Meanwhile, in a small pan over a low heat, slowly reduce the remaining marinade to a thick sauce. Set aside.

Thread 100g (3½oz) of your cabbage pieces onto each of 6 metal skewers.

Light the barbecue. When hot, cook the skewers for about 5 minutes on each side to get a deep caramelisation, turning as needed. Arrange on a plate and finish with a drizzle of the reduced marinade.

Cipollini Onion Skewers

Cipollini are a type of flattish, Italian onion. If you can't find them, a good alternative would be larger silverskin (pearl) onions. The onion barbecue sauce is a super tasty thing, pulled together with ingredients you're likely to have in your store cupboard. Big thanks to former chef Shane for this creation.

Serves 6

For the miso-braised onions

60g (2¼oz) white miso
600g (1lb 5oz) cipollini onions (about 18 onions), peeled but left whole
1 tsp Green Oil (see page 38), to serve

For the onion barbecue sauce

1¾ tbsp date molasses
3 tbsp pomegranate molasses
40g (1½oz) smoked harissa
a splash of red wine vinegar
¾ tsp Ras el Hanout (see page 42)
1 tbsp wholegrain mustard
large pinch of table salt

6 metal or wooden skewers (if using wooden, soak them in water for 30 minutes before use to prevent burning)

For the miso-braised onions, preheat the oven to 170°C/150°C fan/335°F/Gas mark 3½. Combine the miso with 350ml (12fl oz) of water and pour this into a roasting tray. Add the onions with the root ends facing down. Cover the tin with foil and roast for 30 minutes. Leave to cool, then chill the onions in the miso stock overnight.

For the onion barbecue sauce, combine all the ingredients in a bowl. Set aside.

Take the onions out of the stock and thread 3 onions each onto 6 skewers. Put the skewers on a lipped baking tray and brush with the onion barbecue sauce.

Light the barbecue. When hot, cook the skewers, turning regularly to ensure even cooking until they are nicely caramelised, about 10 minutes.

Serve with a spoonful of the barbecue sauce and drizzle over the green oil.

Turnip Skewers with Ras el Hanout

Our executive chef, Ben, was developing a new skewer for the menu and was creating a take on char siu. This evolved into the glaze we used below, as we reached for spices from our dry stores. As it cooks, the edges get beautifully charred, while the middle of the skewer stays super-juicy.

Serves 6

600g (1lb 5oz) turnips (about 2½ large)
2 tsp Harissa Salt (see page 43)
1 lime, cut into wedges

For the marinade
3 tbsp agave nectar
50g (1¾oz) shallot
5 tbsp soy sauce
50g (1¾oz) dates, stones (pits) removed
5 tsp Ras el Hanout (see page 42)
4 tsp merlot vinegar
5 cloves of garlic
1 tbsp smoked paprika

6 metal or wooden skewers (if using wooden, soak them in water for 30 minutes before use to prevent burning)

Slice the turnips finely (a mandolin is useful here), then put them in a mixing bowl with the harissa salt. Leave for at least 1 hour to soften, then scrape off and discard the excess salt and any juice. Cut the slices in quarters, and thread them, packed tightly onto 6 metal skewers, using about 100g (3½oz) per skewer.

For the marinade, place all the ingredients and 2 tablespoons plus 2 teaspoons of water in a blender or mini food processor and blend until completely smooth, about 2 minutes.

Put the skewers on a lipped baking tray and brush with the marinade. Light the barbecue. When hot, cook the skewers until the edges char and the marinade becomes nice and sticky. You will need to turn the skewers while cooking, and continue brushing regularly with more marinade.

Serve on a plate, with a final brush of the reduced marinade and wedges of lime.

Carrot Skewers with Preserved Lemon

There's something quite fun going on here: taking the carrot down and rebuilding it on the skewer. The salt breaks the carrot down enough that it cooks in the relatively short amount of time it's on the grill. This skewer will really change your perception of how a carrot tastes.

Serves 6

650g (1lb 7oz) large carrots (about 9–10 large), peeled
1 tbsp Harissa Salt (see page 43)
4 tbsp Preserved Lemon Purée (see page 200)

For the marinade
1 litre (35fl oz) carrot juice
100g (3½oz) sugar
1 tbsp plus 2 tsp cider vinegar
25g (1oz) rose harissa
½ tsp salt

6 metal or wooden skewers (if using wooden, soak them in water for 30 minutes before use to prevent burning)

Slice the carrots into 5mm (¼in) rounds (a mandolin is useful here) and put in a mixing bowl with the harissa salt. Leave for at least 1 hour to soften, then scrape off and discard the excess salt and any juice.

For the marinade, put the carrot juice and sugar in a high-sided pan. On a high heat, reduce the liquid by two-thirds. The flavour should intensify and the texture will become sticky. This will take about 10 minutes. Stir in the vinegar, rose harissa and salt.

Thread the carrot rounds tightly onto 6 metal skewers, using about 100g (3½oz) for each. Put the skewers on a lipped baking tray and brush with the marinade.

Light the barbecue. When hot, cook the skewers until the edges char and the marinade becomes nice and sticky. You will need to turn the skewers regularly while cooking and continue brushing with more marinade until it is mostly used up.

Serve with a final brush of marinade and a few spoonfuls of the lemon purée.

MAINS

Romano Pepper with Mujadara and Whipped Feta

This is our take on the retro classic of stuffed peppers. Carli, or carliston, peppers are a type of long green pepper that originated in Turkey. If you can't find them, you can use green bell peppers cut into long strips.

It's best to soak the lentils for the mujadara overnight. The onions add so much flavour to the mix, so take your time cooking them down until they are super caramelised. When bringing it all together, season generously with the lemon juice, as it will really lighten up the dish and allow all the other flavours to sing.

Serves 4

4 medium romano peppers (about 800g/1lb 12oz in total)
4 carli peppers (about 200g/7oz in total), or similar long, mild green peppers

For the whipped feta
70g (2½oz) Labneh (see page 60)
70g (2½oz) feta
2 heaped tsp Dijon mustard
¼ tsp salt

For the persillade
3 tbsp Green Oil (see page 38)
1 small shallot, finely diced
5 cloves of garlic, finely diced
a few sprigs of parsley, finely chopped
1 tbsp moscatel vinegar
large pinch of salt
pinch of urfa chilli flakes
pinch of cracked black pepper

For the mujadara freekeh
60g (2¼oz) freekeh
30g (1oz) dried beluga lentils, soaked in water overnight
20g (¾oz) butter
2 tsp vegetable oil
½ white onion, diced
pinch of cumin seeds
pinch of coriander seeds
pinch of ground turmeric
pinch of ground cinnamon
1 tbsp chopped chives
juice of ½ lemon
sea salt and freshly ground black pepper

For the whipped feta, put all the ingredients in a blender and blend until the cheeses combine into one silky-smooth mixture, about 2 minutes. Do not overwhip, or the feta will collapse into a liquid. Set aside.

For the persillade, mix all the ingredients together in a bowl and set aside.

For the mujadara, cook the freekeh and lentils according to package instructions until soft still with a little bite. In a separate pan, gently heat the butter and vegetable oil, add the onion, season with a large pinch of salt and cook on a low heat until sweet and golden. Add all the spices and cook for 1 minute. Fold the cooked grains into the onion, mix in the chives and lemon juice, then taste and adjust the seasoning as needed. Set aside.

To finish, preheat the oven to 170°C/150°C fan/335°F/Gas mark 3½. If you have a kitchen blow-torch, use it to blacken the skins of the romano and carli peppers. Alternatively, using tongs, cook them over an open flame on a gas hob (stovetop), turning until the skins are completely blistered all over. Set the carli peppers aside. For the romano peppers, slice off the tops and remove and discard the seeds, keeping the peppers whole. Stuff the romano peppers with the mujadara freekeh.

Increase the oven temperature to 210°C/190°C fan/410°F/Gas mark 6½. Roast the peppers for about 20 minutes, until they are heated through. To serve, spread the whipped feta on the base of a plate, top with the peppers and dress with the persillade.

Beetroot with Black Garlic Tahini and Sesame Crunch

A Ben Rand classic. Sweet, earthy beetroot (beets) meets the deep umami of our black garlic tahini in this bold dish. Finished with a sesame crunch for texture and nuttiness, it's all about contrast – soft and crisp, rich and sharp. A vibrant plate that's as satisfying as it is striking.

Serves 4

500g (1lb 2oz) baby beetroot (beets) with tops (about 2 bunches)
1 tsp salt
1 tbsp merlot vinegar
1 tbsp toasted sesame oil
50g (1¾oz) Sesame Crumb (see page 43)
100g (3½oz) Black Garlic Tahini (see page 39)

For the crispy leaves
rapeseed (canola) oil, for frying
1 heaped tsp finely sliced beetroot leaves, from above (if not enough, add some kale leaves)
1 tsp dried, ground wakame seaweed

For the pickled stems
beetroot stems (from the beetroot, above)
2 tbsp red wine vinegar
30g (1oz) caster (superfine) sugar
1 tsp toasted sesame oil

For the beetroot (beets), remove and separate the leaves and stems and set aside. Rinse the beetroot, put in a pan, cover with cold water and add the salt. Bring to the boil, turn down the heat and simmer for 25–35 minutes, until completely cooked through. Test with a knife, the tip of which will go in easily when they are done. Drain and set aside in a bowl to cool. Once cool, peel, drizzle with the vinegar and sesame oil and set aside.

For the crispy leaves, pour rapeseed (canola) oil to a depth of 5cm (2in) into a heavy-based pan and heat to 180°C (360°F). Check with a digital probe thermometer, or test by dropping a couple of leaves in. If they bubble and sizzle, the oil is ready. Fry the leaves until crispy, then scoop out, drain on a plate lined with paper towels and season with salt and the dried, ground wakame powder. Set aside.

For the pickled stems, cut the beetroot stems into 5mm (¼in) pieces and put in a heatproof bowl. Put all the other pickling ingredients in a pan with 2 tablespoons of water and bring to the boil. Pour the pickling mixture over the stems and leave to cool in the liquid.

Preheat the grill (broiler). When hot, grill the beetroot until the sugars in the beetroot start to caramelise and the edges start to char, 5–10 minutes. Alternatively, grill the beetroot on a hot barbecue.

Coat the grilled beetroot in the sesame crumb until fully covered. Spread the black garlic tahini in a large bowl and pile the beetroot on top. Dress with the pickled stems and fried leaves and serve.

Celeriac with Fried Capers and Café de Paris

Celeriac, often overlooked in the vegetable world, is a true hidden gem. With its nutty, slightly sweet flavour and creamy texture, it has the versatility to shine in both rustic and refined dishes. When roasted, its edges caramelise beautifully, while the inside remains tender and buttery. This dish takes celeriac to new heights by pairing it with Café de Paris sauce – a rich and aromatic butter sauce from classic French cuisine.

This is a really simple but wholesome main, best served with a portion of Potato Latkes (see page 194) and one of our bitter leaf salads.

Serves 4

1 large celeriac (celery root) (about 600g/1lb 5oz), peeled and trimmed but left whole
2 tbsp olive oil
1 tsp flaky sea salt
1 tbsp rapeseed (canola) oil
35g (1¼oz) capers
4 tsp double (heavy) cream
½ tbsp chives
½ tbsp picked tarragon leaves
4 tsp fresh lemon juice

For the Café de Paris sauce
1 banana shallot (about 75g/2½oz), finely diced
1 clove of garlic, finely diced
2 tbsp rapeseed oil
1 tsp cayenne pepper
2 tsp curry powder
2 tsp mustard powder
160ml (5¼fl oz) double cream
½ tsp flaky sea salt

For the burnt butter
30g (1oz) unsalted butter
pinch of smoked paprika
pinch of table salt

Preheat the oven to 180°C/160°C fan/350°F/Gas mark 4. Coat the celeriac (celery root) with the olive oil, season with the salt, put in a roasting tin and roast for about 90 minutes. Check with a knife. It should pass through the celeriac easily when it's ready.

Meanwhile, for the Café de Paris sauce, gently fry the shallot and garlic in a pan with the rapeseed oil, then add the spices. Cook for 5–8 minutes, stirring regularly, then add the cream and simmer for a further 10 minutes. Taste and season with salt as needed.

For the burnt butter, melt the butter in a pan set over a medium heat. As it begins to foam, whisk until it gives off a nutty aroma and takes on a brown colour, then take off the heat. Strain the butter into a small bowl (discard the solids), then season with the smoked paprika and salt.

Heat 1 tablespoon of rapeseed oil in a small pan. When hot, fry the capers until just crispy. Scoop out with a slotted spoon and drain on a plate lined with paper towels.

To finish the dish, heat the grill (broiler). When hot, grill the roasted celeriac for a few minutes until it has a nice char. Transfer to a large serving plate.

Add the burnt butter mixture to the Café de Paris sauce along with the cream, herbs and lemon juice. Taste and season, then spoon the sauce over the celeriac. Garnish with the crispy capers.

Saffron-braised Fennel with Harissa Labneh, Pistachio and Cranberry

By braising the fennel in butter and saffron, it loses some of its aniseed notes, which are known to often divide its eater. The result is a soft, buttery bulb that works wonderfully with a spicy and aromatic labneh.

Serves 4

2 large or 3 small fennel bulbs (about 750g/1lb 10oz in total)
1 tbsp dried cranberries, chopped
1 tbsp pistachios, chopped
handful of tarragon, leaves coarsely chopped

For the braising liquor
125g (4½oz) unsalted butter
100g (3½oz) caster (superfine) sugar
2 tsp table salt
a few strands of saffron
3 tbsp moscatel vinegar

For the harissa and caper labneh
2 tsp capers, drained
130g (4½oz) Labneh (see page 60)
10g (¼oz) harissa
pinch of table salt
1 tsp lemon juice

Preheat the oven to 180°C/160°C fan/350°F/Gas mark 4.

Halve the fennel bulbs lengthways, discarding any tough outer leaves and the edges of the stems. Arrange the halves, cut-sides down, in a roasting tray.

For the braising liquor, bring all the ingredients and 750ml (26fl oz) water to the boil in a saucepan, stirring until the sugar has dissolved. Pour the braising liquor into the roasting tin to cover the fennel. Roast in the oven for 30–45 minutes, until a knife can be easily inserted into each fennel bulb. Remove the fennel and strain the liquid into a deep frying pan (skillet). Reduce by half. Once reduced, add the fennel bulbs back into the pan and glaze with the now sticky cooking liquor.

For the labneh, finely chop the capers and combine with the labneh, harissa, salt and lemon juice until well mixed.

To serve, spoon and spread the labneh into a bowl. Place the fennel on top, drizzle a little of the braising liquor over, then sprinkle with the cranberries, pistachios and tarragon.

Cauliflower with Peanut Tahini and Salsa Macha

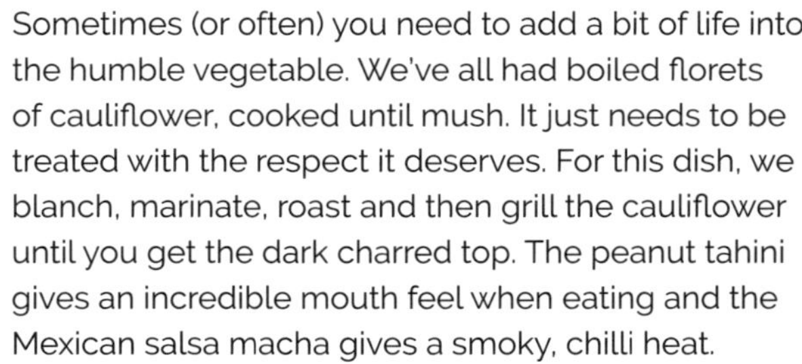
Sometimes (or often) you need to add a bit of life into the humble vegetable. We've all had boiled florets of cauliflower, cooked until mush. It just needs to be treated with the respect it deserves. For this dish, we blanch, marinate, roast and then grill the cauliflower until you get the dark charred top. The peanut tahini gives an incredible mouth feel when eating and the Mexican salsa macha gives a smoky, chilli heat.

Serves 4

1 large cauliflower (about 800g/1lb 12oz), trimmed, leaves discarded
100ml (3½fl oz) roasted cauliflower marinade (from recipe below)
1 tbsp lemon juice
1 tbsp chopped fresh coriander (cilantro), to serve
pinch of flaky sea salt

For the roasted cauliflower marinade

2½ tsp cumin seeds
1½ tsp coriander seeds
1 large dried black lime
2 tbsp plus 2 tsp rapeseed (canola) oil
1 tbsp red wine vinegar
1 tbsp plus 1 tsp agave nectar
1 tsp flaky sea salt

For the peanut tahini

1½ tsp white miso paste
20g (¾oz) smooth peanut butter
2 tbsp plus 1 tsp lime juice
½ tsp tamari soy sauce
70g (2½oz) tahini
4 tsp maple syrup

For the marinade, toast the cumin and coriander seeds in a dry pan until fragrant. Finely grind in a spice grinder, then add the black lime and finely grind again. Transfer to a bowl, add all the remaining marinade ingredients and whisk until fully blended.

Heat the oven to 250°C/230°C fan/480°F/Gas mark 10. Fill a large bowl with iced water and line a roasting tray with baking paper.

Bring a medium pan of salted water to the boil and blanch the cauliflower for 8 minutes, then scoop out and refresh in the iced water. Drain thoroughly and transfer the cauliflower to the prepared roasting tray.

Coat the cauliflower with the marinade, making sure to give it a good stir before using. Roast in the oven for 20–30 minutes, or until golden and caramelised.

Meanwhile, for the peanut tahini, put the miso, peanut butter, lime juice and tamari in a mixing bowl and use an electric hand whisk to bring the ingredients together until smooth and emulsified, then add the tahini and maple syrup. Whisk until smooth, then add 3 tbsp plus 2 tsp cold water, whisking again until fully incorporated. Season to taste with salt and set aside.

Recipe continued overleaf...

For the salsa macha

¼ tsp cumin seeds
15g (½oz) sesame seeds
25g (1oz) pumpkin seeds
pinch of ground allspice
3 tbsp plus 2 tsp olive oil (garlic oil from the Confit Garlic, see page 47, is ideal)
25g (1oz) smoked harissa
pinch of flaky sea salt

For the salsa macha, keeping them separate, toast the cumin, sesame and pumpkin seeds in a dry pan until golden and fragrant. Grind each separately, transfer to a bowl, add the rest of the ingredients and whisk until well combined. Set aside.

To finish the dish, heat the grill (broiler). When hot, grill the roasted cauliflower for a few minutes until lightly charred. Smooth the peanut tahini on a serving plate, then top with the cauliflower. Drizzle over the salsa macha and lemon juice, then garnish with the coriander and a sprinkle of flaky sea salt.

Carrots, Peanut Tahini, Coconut and Lime Leaf Salsa

Roasted carrots get a bold lift from creamy peanut tahini in this dish of rich, nutty, and deeply savoury flavours. The coconut and lime leaf salsa adds brightness and fragrance, cutting through with a fresh, zesty punch. A dish that's rooted in comfort, but full of surprises.

Serves 4

For the Jerusalem spice mix
¼ tsp cumin seeds
¼ tsp coriander seeds
¼ cardamom pod
⅛ tsp ground turmeric

For the roasted carrots
1 tbsp cumin seeds
2 tsp fennel seeds
250g (9oz) leafy carrots, tops removed, scrubbed and trimmed to leave 2.5cm (1in) of the green stems (prepared weight)
1 tbsp rapeseed (canola) oil
flaky sea salt

Preheat the oven to 180°C/160°C fan/350°F/Gas mark 4.

To make the Jerusalem spice mix, toast the cumin seeds, coriander seeds and cardamom pod in a dry pan until fragrant. Transfer to a pestle and mortar or a spice grinder, add the turmeric and grind to a coarse powder. Set aside.

For the roasted carrots, toast the cumin seeds and fennel seeds in a dry pan until fragrant, then grind. Toss the carrots in the oil and spices, season with a large pinch of flaky sea salt and transfer to a large roasting tray. Roast for about 25 minutes, or until cooked but still a little al dente.

Meanwhile, for the coconut and lime leaf salsa, toast the coconut in a dry pan until golden. Set aside. Put the green chilli in a blender with the garlic and lime leaves. Blend for 2 minutes, or until it reaches a smooth paste consistency.

Once smooth, add the coriander, lime juice, Jerusalem spice mix, flaky sea salt, tamari and agave nectar and blend again. When smooth, add the oil and blend to form a smooth, emulsified sauce. Taste and check the seasoning, adjusting as needed. Set aside.

Recipe continued overleaf...

For the coconut and lime leaf salsa

1 tbsp desiccated (dried shredded) coconut
½ small green chilli, deseeded and roughly chopped
1 clove of garlic
2 lime leaves, finely sliced
30g (1oz) fresh coriander (cilantro) leaves, roughly chopped
2 tsp lime juice
1 tsp Jerusalem spice mix (see above)
1½ tbsp flaky sea salt
2 tsp tamari soy sauce
1 tsp agave nectar
2 tbsp plus 2 tsp rapeseed oil

For the peanut tahini

1 heaped tsp white miso paste
20g (¾oz) smooth peanut butter
2 tbsp plus 1 tsp lime juice
1 tsp tamari soy sauce
70g (2½oz) tahini
4 tsp maple syrup

For the peanut tahini, put the miso, peanut butter, lime juice and tamari in a mixing bowl. Using an electric hand whisk, blend to form a smooth, emulsified sauce, then add the tahini and maple syrup. Whisk all the ingredients together until smooth, then add 3 tablespoons plus 2 teaspoons of cold water and whisk until fully incorporated. Taste and season.

To finish the carrots, heat a grill (broiler). When hot, grill the roasted carrots in a single layer, turning, to give them a little char. To serve, smooth the peanut tahini over a large plate, arrange the carrots on top and spoon over the salsa. Sprinkle with the toasted coconut and finish with a pinch of flaky sea salt.

Celeriac Musakhan

This is a twist on the beloved Palestinian dish, musakhan, which is known for its bold flavours of sumac, caramelised onions and warm spices. We have given the celeriac a sweet miso glaze and served it with the musakhan-style onions on a velvety bed of tahini. A simple, winter warmer.

Serves 4

1 large celeriac (celery root) (about 600g/1lb 5oz), peeled and trimmed
150ml (5fl oz) Tahini Sauce (see page 38)
1½ tbsp chopped parsley
scant tsp sumac

For the sweet, spiced miso glaze
20g (¾oz) white miso paste
¼ tsp aleppo chilli flakes
scant tsp agave nectar
½ tbsp rice wine vinegar
1 clove of Confit Garlic (see page 47)
¼ tsp lemon juice
½ tsp sweet spice/ground mixed spice
1 tbsp plus 2 tsp rapeseed (canola) oil

For the musakhan onions
1 large white onion (about 185g/6½oz)
4 tsp olive oil
½ tsp flaky sea salt
1 tbsp sumac
2 tsp sugar
¾ tsp lemon juice

For the sweet spiced miso glaze, put all the glaze ingredients, except the oil, in a blender and blitz until smooth. Slowly drizzle in the oil, blending between additions, until you have a smooth, emulsified sauce.

For the musakhan onions, finely slice the onion and put in a pan with the olive oil and salt, then cook very gently, uncovered, until pale golden and really soft and jammy. This will take 30–40 minutes. Add the sumac, sugar and lemon juice and season to taste.

Slice the celeriac into 1.5cm (½in) rounds – it should make 4–6 slices.

Preheat the oven to 180°C/160°C fan/350°F/Gas mark 4 and switch to the grill (broiler) setting once the temperature is met, Grill the celeriac (celery root) on all sides until nicely charred, then brush the miso glaze on the cut side, return the oven and roast the celeriac until the glaze is caramelised, about 20–30 minutes, or until completely soft when tested with a knife.

Smooth the tahini sauce onto a serving plate and arrange the musakhan onions on top, along with the celeriac. Garnish with the parsley and sumac, and an extra sprinkle of flaky sea salt.

Grezzina Courgette, Tarator and Tomato Jam

We use *grezzina* courgettes (zucchini), a pale-skinned variety with denser flesh and fewer seeds – the type you tend to see on holiday in southern Europe. If you're unable to get these, then buy the smallest, firmest courgettes you can find.

In the restaurant, we smoke the tomatoes prior to making the jam; this adds another layer of intensity, but the jam is still delicious if this stage is missed. If you wanted to add this step at home, see page 22. You'll end up with more tomato jam here, but it's a wonderful condiment to have in your fridge!

Serves 4

8 *grezzina* courgettes (about 250g/9oz in total); you can use 4–6 ordinary courgettes if unavailable
coarse salt
rapeseed (canola) oil, for brushing

For the tomato jam (Makes 125g/4½oz)

400g (14oz) tomatoes – vine or datterini mix
2 tbsp merlot vinegar
½ tsp extra virgin olive oil
1 tsp urfa chilli flakes
½ heaped tsp harissa
½ tsp salt
⅛ shallot, finely chopped
½ tbsp chopped chives

To serve

150g (5½oz) Tarator (see page 39)
10g (¼oz) House Za'atar (see page 40)
a few sprigs of oregano

Roll the courgettes in a plate of the coarse salt so the skin is punctured. Set aside for 45 minutes, then wash the salt off.

Put the 400g (14oz) whole tomatoes in a large frying pan (skillet) set over a medium heat, adding the vinegar, olive oil, chilli flakes, harissa and salt. Cook, stirring, until the tomatoes have broken down, thickened and taken on a jam-like consistency. This will take about 20 minutes.

Add the shallot and chives to the jam pan. Set aside. This recipe makes more tomato jam than you will need for the recipe. Store the remainder in the fridge for up to 1 week.

Brush the courgettes with rapeseed oil and preheat the grill. When hot, grill for 5–10 minutes, or until nicely charred, brushing with more oil halfway through if needed.

To a serve, spoon the tomato jam and tarator onto a plate, top with the courgettes, sprinkle with za'atar and garnish with the oregano sprigs.

Onion Squash with Red and Green Zhoug and Kataifi

During our pop-up series for Bubala's fifth birthday, we collaborated on a dinner with the team from Legare, an Italian restaurant in London. They brought an incredible double-concentrated tomato purée (tomato paste) from Sicily, which we incorporated into a red zhoug and served with our latkes. We remembered this when onion squash came into season. Although delicious, it needed more to be a main, so we added a fresh, green zhoug, some crunch, and then the date chutney. Voilà!

The zhougs, chutney and crumble can all be made ahead to simplify the cooking process. You'll end up with more of them here than you need, but they're all wonderful things to have in the fridge. We use onion squash, a dense, sweet-fleshed squash. It also creates a pleasing boat shape when quartered, allowing it to hold the sauce, but any other variety of squash or pumpkin would work.

Serves 4

1 large onion squash
pinch of flaky sea salt
pinch of cracked black pepper
1 tbsp olive oil

For the green zhoug

½ green chilli, deseeded
30g (1oz) spring onions (scallions), chopped
45g (1½oz) fresh coriander (cilantro), chopped
15g (½oz) parsley, chopped
juice of ½ lime
pinch of cardamom seeds
½ tsp cumin seeds
pinch of sugar
pinch of salt

For the red zhoug

25g (1oz) sun-dried tomatoes
3 tbsp plus 1 tsp boiling water
2 tbsp plus 2 tsp rapeseed (canola) oil
45g (1½oz) red chilli, finely chopped
25g (1oz) garlic, finely chopped

For the green zhoug, using tongs, char the green chilli on an open flame on a gas hob (stovetop) until blistered all over. Place the charred chilli and all the other green zhoug ingredients in a blender and blend until smooth. Set aside in a piping bag or squeeze-top sauce bottle.

For the red zhoug, put the sun-dried tomatoes in a small heatproof bowl and pour over the boiling water to cover. Set aside. Heat the rapeseed oil and fry the chopped chilli and garlic until golden, then add the spices and tomato purée (tomato paste). Transfer to a blender, add the soaked sun-dried tomatoes and their water and blend until smooth. Set aside in a piping bag or squeeze-top sauce bottle. This recipe makes more of the red and green zhoug than you will need. Store the rest in the fridge for up to 3 days.

For the date and sesame chutney, toast the sesame seeds in a dry pan until golden and aromatic. Set aside. Blend the remaining chutney ingredients in a blender until smooth, then fold in the sesame seeds. Set aside.

Recipe continued overleaf...

pinch of ground turmeric
½ clove
2 cardamom pods
½ tsp smoked paprika
¼ tsp cumin seeds
1 tsp lemon juice
25g (1oz) tomato purée (tomato paste)

For the date and sesame chutney
30g (1oz) sesame seeds
20g (¾oz) Confit Garlic (about 7 cloves; see page 47)
15g (½oz) white miso paste
2¾ tsp date syrup

For the sesame and paprika crumble
2 tbsp white sesame seeds
2 tbsp black sesame seeds
1 tsp smoked paprika
pinch of flaky sea salt
¼ tsp soft brown sugar

For the kataifi crunch
rapeseed oil for deep frying
75g (2½oz) kataifi pastry
15g (½oz) wild rice
1 tsp sesame and paprika crumble (from the recipe above)
2 tbsp chopped fresh coriander (cilantro)

For the sesame and paprika crumble, toast both types of sesame seed in a dry pan until golden and aromatic. Transfer to a blender and pulse with the remaining crumble ingredients, until a coarse crumble consistency is reached. Set aside.

For the kataifi crunch, half-fill a deep, heavy-based pan with the rapeseed oil and heat to 180°C (360°F). A digital probe thermometer is useful here but if you don't have one, the oil is ready when a small piece of kataifi sizzles when it hits the hot oil. Pull the kataifi apart into threads, and fry in the hot oil until it stops bubbling. Scoop out onto a plate lined with paper towels to drain. Set aside.

Drop the wild rice into the same pan of oil and stir with a whisk. Fry until the rice is puffed and crispy, and open like a breakfast cereal. Scoop out and drain on a plate lined with paper towels. In a bowl, combine the kataifi, wild rice, the sesame and paprika crumble and the coriander and mix to combine. Set aside.

For the onion squash, preheat the oven to 190°C/170°C fan/375°F/Gas mark 5. Cut the squash in half, from the stem to the core. Scoop out the seeds and cut the halves into 3 wedges. Put in a roasting tray and season with salt, cracked black pepper and olive oil. Cover the roasting tray with foil, so the squash will steam-roast. Cook for 30–40 minutes, or until soft throughout when tested with a knife.

To serve, pipe the red zhoug in a tight zigzag pattern over a large serving plate, then repeat with the green zhoug, so the pattern alternates between green and red. Pile the kataifi crunch on top, arrange the squash on the plate and serve with the date and sesame chutney.

Cauliflower with Sunflower Seed and Sambal

A whole-roasted and dressed cauliflower is an impressive thing, sitting proudly on the table. The sunflower seed sambal involves slowly roasting the sunflower seeds in a spicy, garlicky oil, and the result is a deep and complex sauce.

The inner core of the cauliflower can be hard to get to when you are trying to impart flavour into the whole vegetable. That's where brining comes in, which gives lots of additional flavour from the aromatics in the liquid. You can also smoke the cauliflower after brining, to impart further flavour, if you like – you can read about smoking on page 22.

Serves 4

1 large cauliflower (about 900g/2lb), trimmed, tough outer leaves removed
2.3 litres (78fl oz) Brining Liquid (see page 45)
handful of fresh mint leaves

For the sunflower seed purée
100g (3½oz) sunflower seeds
1 tbsp rapeseed (canola) oil
3 cloves of garlic
1 tsp smoked paprika
1 tsp black peppercorns
1 tbsp lemon juice
½ tsp table salt

For the tamarind water
1 tbsp plus 2 tsp boiling water
1 tsp tamarind pulp

For the sunflower seed sambal
50g (1¾oz) onion, chopped
3 cloves of garlic
25g (1oz) red chilli
3 tbsp plus 1 tsp vegetable oil
50g (1¾oz) sunflower seeds
2 tbsp tamarind water (see above)
1 tsp caster (superfine) sugar
½ tsp flaky sea salt

Put the cauliflower in a deep roasting tray. Pour the brining liquid over until fully covered and leave to brine overnight.

The next morning, drain the cauliflower and fill a large bowl with iced water. Bring a large pan of salted water to the boil, add the cauliflower and boil for about 10 minutes, or until tender when tested with the tip of a knife. Scoop out the cauliflower and refresh in the iced water, then set aside.

For the sunflower seed purée, put the sunflower seeds in a pan with water to cover, bring to the boil, then simmer for about 1 hour, or until the seeds are completely soft. Drain.

Heat the oil in a pan over a medium heat, add the garlic and cook, stirring, until golden brown and caramelised, 5–10 minutes. Transfer the garlic and all the remaining purée ingredients, except the lemon juice and salt, to a blender with 125ml (4fl oz) of water and blend until smooth. Season with the lemon juice and salt and set aside.

For the tamarind water, pour the boiling water into a small pan and drop in the tamarind pulp. Use a whisk to break up the pulp as it cools, then strain through a fine sieve (sifter) and discard the remnants. Set aside.

For the sunflower seed sambal, blend the onion, garlic and chilli to a paste in a blender. Heat the vegetable oil in a wide pan set over a medium heat, then add the onion, garlic and

Recipe continued overleaf...

For the cauliflower barbecue sauce

130g (4½oz) sunflower seed purée (from recipe above)
4 tbsp plus 2 tsp tamarind water (from recipe above)
1½ tsp demerara (light brown) sugar

chilli paste and the sunflower seeds. Leave to cook slowly, stirring frequently so it doesn't catch on the base of the pan, for about 40 minutes, or until there is no taste of raw garlic or onion left. Let it cool slightly, then add the tamarind water and season with sugar and salt. Set aside.

For the barbecue sauce, put all the ingredients in a blender and blend until smooth, until you have a loose cream consistency. Brush the cauliflower with all of the barbecue sauce, until covered completely.

Preheat the oven to 230°C/210°C fan/450°F/Gas mark 8. When hot, roast the cauliflower, turning occasionally, to get a nice caramelization, 25–35 minutes. Finish with a squeeze of lemon and a pinch of flaky sea salt.

To serve, spoon the remaining sunflower seed purée onto a large plate, top with the cauliflower, followed by the sambal and garnish with mint leaves. Any leftover sambal can be stored, covered in the fridge, for up to 3 days.

Carrots, Tamarind Yoghurt and Vadouvan Butter

Sweet, roasted carrots meet tangy tamarind yoghurt for a hit of sharpness and creaminess. A drizzle of vadouvan butter – spiced, rich, and fragrant – brings it all together. It's a dish that plays with depth and contrast, with familiar flavours turned on their head. Just what Helen planned.

Serves 4

1 tbsp cumin seeds, toasted in a dry pan until fragrant
2 tsp fennel seeds, toasted in a dry pan until fragrant
1 tbsp rapeseed (canola) oil
8 medium carrots with their leafy tops, scrubbed and trimmed to leave 2.5cm (1in) of the green stems
2 tsp lemon juice
flaky sea salt
handful of curry leaves, fried until crisp in rapeseed oil, to serve

For the vadouvan butter

50g (1¾oz) dates, stones (pits) removed
1 heaped tsp table salt
4 tbsp vadouvan curry powder
200g (7oz) unsalted butter
1 tsp moscatel vinegar
1 tbsp lemon juice

For the tamarind yoghurt

100g (3½oz) Labneh (see page 60), or thick Greek yoghurt
30g (1oz) tamarind paste
scant tbsp date syrup
zest of ½ unwaxed lime

Preheat the oven to 180°C/160°C fan/350°F/Gas mark 4.

Grind the cumin and fennel seeds in a mortar and pestle or spice grinder, then combine with the oil and a pinch of flaky sea salt. Put the carrots in a roasting tin and toss them in the spice mixture. Roast for about 25 minutes, or until cooked but still al dente.

Meanwhile, for the vadouvan butter, slice the dates finely and put in a heatproof bowl with the salt and curry powder. Melt the butter in a saucepan set over a medium heat, whisking until the butter solids have separated out and caramelised on the base of the pan, and the butter has a light hazelnut brown colour. This will take about 5 minutes.

Pour the hot caramelised butter over the curry powder and salt, then whisk until fully incorporated. Add the vinegar and lemon juice to the mixture, taste to check the seasoning and set aside. This recipe makes more vadouvan butter than you will need. Keep the remainder in a jar in the fridge for up to 1 week.

For the tamarind yoghurt, combine the labneh with all the other yoghurt ingredients in a bowl until incorporated. Spread the tamarind yoghurt over the base of a large bowl.

To finish the carrots, heat the grill (broiler). When hot, transfer the carrots from the oven to the grill and cook, turning, until they are charred all over. Arrange them over the tamarind yoghurt.

Heat the vadouvan butter and stir through the 2 teaspoons of lemon juice, then spoon this over the carrots adding a pinch of flaky sea salt. Garnish with the fried curry leaves to serve.

Braised Hispi, Whipped Tofu, Chive and Ginger Salsa, Ponzu

This dish nods to Southeast Asia with its bright, punchy flavours of ginger, chive, and citrusy ponzu layered over tender, braised hispi cabbage. The whipped tofu adds a gentle, cooling contrast, letting the bold salsa shine. Light, vibrant, and full of energy. You can store any remaining ponzu or chive salsa, covered in the fridge, for up to 3 days.

Serves 4

1 hispi cabbage, tough outer layers peeled and discarded, cut into 2–3 even chunks
rapeseed (canola) oil, for brushing
1.5 litres (50fl oz) Burnt Vegetable Stock (see page 45)
flaky sea salt

For the ponzu
2 tbsp mirin
2 tbsp rice vinegar
120ml (3¾fl oz) tamari soy sauce
4 tbsp lemon juice
4 tbsp orange juice

For the chive salsa
1 tbsp sesame seeds
1 whole white peppercorn
3 tbsp (1oz) fresh coriander (cilantro) leaves
4 tbsp (1¾oz) chopped chives
10g (¼oz) fresh root ginger
2 tbsp plus 2 tsp rapeseed oil
1 tbsp tamari soy sauce

For the whipped tofu
210g (7½oz) pack silken tofu
2 tsp toasted sesame oil
pinch of table salt
4 tsp rapeseed oil

Preheat the oven to 180°C/160°C fan/350°F/Gas mark 4.

Heat a dry frying pan (skillet) over a high heat until it is very hot. Brush the cabbage pieces with rapeseed oil and place cut-side down in the pan. Char and caramelise the cabbage, turning to char the other cut sides, then transfer to a roasting dish or tray. Pour over the burnt vegetable stock so the pieces are three-quarters submerged. Sprinkle over a little flaky sea salt and cover the dish tightly with foil. Roast for 40 minutes, or until the cabbage is tender and cooked through. Strain and discard the liquid, reduce the oven temperature to 100°C/80°C fan/210°F/Gas mark ¼ and return the cabbage to the warm oven.

Meanwhile, for the ponzu, whisk all the ingredients together in a bowl and set aside.

For the chive salsa, toast the sesame seeds in a dry pan until golden and fragrant, then cool and transfer to a heatproof bowl. Grind the white peppercorn and add to the bowl. Finely chop the coriander leaves and chives and add them to the bowl, then finely grate the ginger (a Microplane is useful here) and add it too. Heat the oil in a small pan over a high heat until just smoking, then pour over all the ingredients in the bowl. Once cool, stir in the tamari.

For the whipped tofu, blend all the ingredients in a blender, except the rapeseed oil until well combined. Slowly add the rapeseed oil, blending well between additions, until the whipped tofu is glossy and smooth.

To serve, spoon the whipped tofu into a bowl, add the braised cabbage, and top with the chive salsa and ponzu to your liking.

Braised Cabbage with Romesco and Seaweed Crunch

This is a dish that Alexis, our Head Chef at Bubala Spitalfields, put on the menu. It's colourful and full of flavour. We use the best hazelnuts you can get – Italy's finest Piedmont hazelnuts – which are renowned for their exceptional sweetness, delicate aroma, and crisp texture. The leftover seaweed crunch and romesco would be great additions to your Bubies wrap (see pages 28–31).

Serves 4

1 head of Savoy cabbage
3 tbsp rapeseed (canola) oil
1.5 litres (50fl oz) Burnt Vegetable Stock (see page 45)
2 tbsp lemon juice
a few sprigs of parsley
pinch of urfa chilli flakes
flaky sea salt

For the seaweed crunch
30g (1oz) golden sultanas (golden raisins)
10g (¼oz) nori sheets (about 3 sheets)
20g (¾oz) pumpkin seeds
2 tbsp rapeseed oil
35g (1¼oz) shallots, sliced
3 cloves of garlic, sliced
4 tsp tamari soy sauce
120ml (3¾fl oz) Confit Garlic oil (see Confit Garlic, page 47)
1½ tsp toasted sesame oil

Preheat the oven to 180°C/160°C fan/350°F/Gas mark 4.

For the seaweed crunch, soak the golden sultanas in warm water for about 1 hour, then strain and set aside in a bowl (keep warm).

Cut the savoy cabbage into 4 equal portions, making sure to cut through the core so the pieces stay intact. Heat a frying pan (skillet) over a high heat until very hot, then brush the cabbage with the rapeseed oil and place cut-side down in the pan. Turn to char and caramelise the cut faces of the cabbage, then transfer to a roasting tray. Pour over the stock so the cabbage pieces are three-quarters submerged. Season with a little flaky sea salt and cover tightly with foil. Roast in the oven for 40 minutes, or until the cabbage is tender and cooked through when tested with a knife. Strain and discard the liquid, reduce the oven temperature to 100°C/80°C fan/215°F/Gas mark ¼ and return the cabbage to the oven to keep warm.

While the cabbage is roasting, make the other components. To continue with the seaweed crunch, blitz the nori sheets in a blender to a powder. Toast the pumpkin seeds in a dry pan until nicely browned. Heat the rapeseed oil in a pan, then fry the shallots and garlic for a minute or two, until crispy. Scoop out and drain on a plate lined with paper towels. Add the nori, pumpkin seeds and the fried shallots and garlic to the bowl with the sultanas, along with all the other seaweed crunch ingredients. Mix well and set aside.

Recipe continued overleaf...

For the romesco
320g (11¼oz) red (bell) peppers (about 2 medium), or 165g (5¾oz) grilled red (bell) peppers from a jar
25g (1oz) Piedmont hazelnuts, toasted in a dry pan
1 clove of garlic
1 tsp flaky sea salt
½ tsp pomegranate molasses
pinch of cayenne pepper
4 tsp sherry vinegar
1 tsp smoked paprika
5 tbsp plus 1 tsp olive oil

For the romesco, on a barbecue or over an open flame on a gas hob (stovetop), using tongs, grill the peppers until charred on the outside and soft inside. Leave them to cool, then peel them and discard the skins. Put the peppers and all the remaining romesco ingredients in a blender, except the oil. Blend for 1 minute, then slowly add the oil, blending well between additions, to form a smooth, glossy emulsified sauce. Taste and adjust the seasoning if necessary.

To serve, spoon the romesco on the base of the plate, top with the cabbage and a drizzle of lemon, then sprinkle over the seaweed crunch. Garnish with the parsley sprigs, and a sprinkle of chilli flakes and flaky sea salt.

Kohlrabi with Ajo Blanco, Almond and Kumquat Salsa

Kohlrabi is one of those underused vegetables that deserves more of the spotlight – mild, slightly sweet, and perfect when braised until tender. Here, it's paired with a silky ajo blanco (made with almonds soaked overnight) and topped with a sharp, citrusy kumquat and almond salsa. A dish that's understated, elegant, and all about letting great ingredients shine.

Serves 2 generously, serves 4 with a couple of other dishes to share as well

2 large kohlrabi (about 600g/1lb 5oz in total), trimmed, peeled, woody bases removed
2 tsp rapeseed (canola) oil
2 tsp flaky sea salt
2 tsp cracked black pepper
a handful of smoked almonds, chopped, to serve

For the ajo blanco
50g (3½oz) blanched almonds, soaked in 5 tbsp plus 1 tsp water overnight
1 small ice cube
50ml (3½fl oz) olive oil
½ clove of garlic
1 tbsp moscatel vinegar
1 tsp lemon juice
pinch of table salt

Preheat the oven to 180°C/160°C fan/350°F/Gas mark 4.

Put the kohlrabi in a roasting tray, drizzle with the oil and season with the salt and pepper. Roast for 1½ hours, or until you can easily slide a knife into the centres of the kohlrabi, then cool.

Meanwhile, for the ajo blanco, strain the soaked almonds, reserving the soaking water, then blitz the almonds with the ice cube in a blender to a fine paste. Slowly add the soaking water and the olive oil, alternating, until you have a smooth, emulsified sauce, scraping down the sides of the blender with a spatula as you go.

Add the garlic, vinegar, lemon juice and salt and blend until smooth, then taste and adjust the seasoning if needed. The final consistency should be that of a dressing that holds itself on a plate. If it is too stiff, add a splash of water and keep blending until smooth. Set aside.

Recipe continued overleaf...

For the kumquat salsa

5g (1oz) smoked almonds
35g (1¼oz) kumquats, topped and tailed
large handful of picked basil leaves
large handful of picked fresh coriander (cilantro) leaves
1 clove of garlic
2 tsp rice vinegar
2 tsp fresh lemon juice
½ tsp flaky sea salt
scant tsp maple syrup
1½ tsp orange flower water
6 tbsp rapeseed oil

For the kumquat salsa, blitz the smoked almonds in a blender to a chunky consistency, then transfer to a bowl. Halve the kumquats, halve again, then finely slice and add to the bowl with the nuts. Finely slice the basil and coriander and add to the bowl, then add all the other salsa ingredients, mix well and taste to check the seasoning, adjusting as needed.

To serve, slice each kohlrabi into 2cm (¾in) rounds. Spoon the ajo blanco into a serving bowl, arrange the kohlrabi on top, dollop over the kumquat salsa, then top with the chopped smoked almonds.

Ful Medames with Malawach Bread

Ful medames is a traditional Egyptian dish made of stewed beans. It's hearty and perfect for cold winter nights, served with malawach – a flaky, buttery bread to mop up the stew – and a lovage pesto for some added herby zest. The beans will need to be soaked the night before, and you can also make the breads up to two days in advance and reheat.

Serves 4–6

500g (1lb 2oz) dried haricot beans
½ tsp bicarbonate of soda (baking soda)
2 tbsp rapeseed (canola) oil
500g (1lb 2oz) onions, finely chopped
6 cloves of garlic, finely chopped
pinch of ground cumin
¼ tbsp ground cinnamon
½ tsp cayenne pepper
1 tbsp sweet paprika
1 large tomato, grated
zest and juice of 1 unwaxed lemon
yoghurt, to serve (optional)

For the malawach breads (Makes 6)

315ml (10¾fl oz) warm water (about 40°C/105°F)
1 tsp dried yeast
30g (1oz) sugar
500g (1lb 2oz) plain (all-purpose) flour
1 tsp nigella seeds
20g (¾oz) salt
1 tbsp rapeseed oil
250g (9oz) butter, softened

Soak the beans overnight in plenty of water. The next day, put them in a large pan with fresh water to cover generously, add the bicarbonate of soda, bring to the boil, then turn down the heat and simmer until the beans are soft, skimming off any foam that forms on the surface. This will take about 1–2 hours. Drain, reserving the cooking liquid.

Meanwhile, make the malawach breads. In a measuring jug, combine the warm water, yeast and sugar. Mix well to dissolve.

In a large mixing bowl or stand mixer fitted with a dough hook, combine the flour, nigella seeds and salt. Gradually add the water mixture, mixing well between additions, until a soft, sticky dough is formed. Turn the dough out onto a work surface and knead to a smooth and elasticated dough, around 15 minutes. At this point the dough should be tacky but not stick to a clean finger if gently prodded.

Oil a metal tray with half the rapeseed oil. Divide the dough into 6 equal portions (about 130g/4½oz each) and shape into balls. Place on the prepared tray, brushing the remaining oil on top. Loosely cover with cling film (plastic wrap) or a clean dish towel. Leave to rise somewhere warm for 1 hour. The dough will double in size and feel relaxed to the touch.

While the breads are rising, continue with the ful medames and make the lovage pesto. For the ful medames, heat the rapeseed oil in a large pan over a medium heat. When hot, sauté the onions and garlic until soft, then add the spices and continue cooking gently until soft and aromatic, about 15 minutes. Stir this mixture into the drained beans, then divide the bean mixture in half. Put one half in a large pan over a medium heat. Put the other half in a blender with a tablespoon or two of the reserved

Recipe continued overleaf...

For the lovage pesto
2 cloves of garlic
20g (¾oz) lovage
20g (¾oz) basil
15g (½oz) Preserved Lemons (see page 49)
1 tsp lemon juice
25g (1oz) parsley
150ml (5fl oz) olive oil

bean-cooking liquid and the grated tomato and blitz until smooth. Add this blended mixture to the pan with the rest of the beans and continue to simmer gently for 1 hour.

For the lovage pesto, put all the ingredients, except the olive oil, in a blender and blend to a coarse paste. Slowly pour in the oil, blending well between additions, until the mixture is smooth and emulsified. Set aside.

Now to shape the breads. Spread a little of the softened butter on a clean work surface, take one dough ball and gently spread, pulling and stretching it to a rough rectangle about 30 x 15cm (12 x 6in). Using your hands, smear some of the butter over the surface, being mindful not to tear the dough.

Next, take one of the short edges of the dough and fold onto itself, so the edge is now in the centre. Repeat on the other side so you now have a smaller rectangle, then spread more butter on this surface. Working from the bottom edge, roll the dough into a cylinder, flatten, then spread more butter over and roll from the outside edge into a spiral shape.

Place back onto the tray and repeat with the remaining dough balls (you will use nearly all of the butter). Once all are shaped, cover loosely again and allow to prove for 30 minutes at room temperature.

To cook the breads, put one of the proved breads on a lightly oiled work surface and use your fingertips to flatten the dough to a 15cm (6in) circle the thickness of a pound coin.

Heat a 30cm (12in) frying pan (skillet) on a medium heat. Add a little butter, and when it starts to foam, add the bread and cook for 5 minutes on one side, then turn it over and give it another 5 minutes. Repeat with the remaining breads, keeping each warm while you cook the others.

The breads can also be baked. Preheat the oven to 255°C/235°C fan/490°F/Gas mark 9 with the baking trays inside. When the trays are hot, place the flattened breads on them and bake for 15–20 minutes, or until they are dark golden, crispy and light.

When the breads are cooked and you're ready to serve, taste the bean mixture, adding the lemon juice and zest, and salt to taste. Serve in bowls with a generous spoonful of lovage pesto and malawach on the side, plus yoghurt if liked. Leftover lovage pesto can be kept covered in the fridge for up to 3 days.

Aubergine, Peanut and Curry Leaf Crunch

This dish by our Executive Chef, Ben, is so good that it stayed on the menu for months! On paper, this dish may look quite daunting, but most of the work sits in the preparation, making it a great option if you're entertaining. The aubergine (eggplant) does need to be marinated the day before, or for at least 6 hours.

Serves 4

2 medium aubergines (eggplant)
1 tbsp lime juice, to serve
2 tbsp chopped fresh coriander (cilantro) leaves, to serve

For the aubergine marinade (Makes 250ml/9fl oz)
50g (1¾oz) white miso
1 tbsp plus 2 tsp tamari soy sauce
25g (1oz) tahini
1 small clove of garlic
½ tsp caster (superfine) sugar
¼ tsp toasted sesame oil
3 tbsp plus 1 tsp Dashi Stock (see page 44)

For the peanut sauce
35g (1¼oz) peanuts
2 tsp agave nectar
100ml (3½fl oz) aubergine marinade (from recipe above)

For the curry leaf crunch
rapeseed (canola) oil, for shallow frying
125g (4½oz) shallot, sliced in rings
1 bulb of garlic (about 20 cloves), sliced
15g (½oz) fresh curry leaves
35g (1¼oz) roasted peanuts, crushed (see method for roasting instructions)

For the marinade, blend all the marinade ingredients in a blender until completely smooth. Set aside 100ml (3½fl oz), which will be used to make the peanut sauce.

On a barbecue or over an open flame on a gas hob (stovetop), using tongs, grill the aubergines until charred on the outside and totally soft inside. Leave them to cool, then peel, discard the skins, but leave the stems intact. Transfer to a bowl, cover with the remaining marinade and leave to marinate, covered in the fridge, for at least 6 hours, or ideally overnight.

For the peanut sauce, line a baking tray with baking paper and roast the peanuts for 15–20 minutes, until golden brown. Allow to cool, then transfer to a blender, add the agave nectar and the reserved marinade and blend until smooth, 3–5 minutes. Set aside.

For the curry leaf crunch, heat 2cm (¾in) of rapeseed oil in a heavy-based pan. When hot, individually shallow fry the shallot, garlic and curry leaves until crispy, scooping each out and draining on a plate lined with paper towels. Transfer the fried shallot, garlic and curry leaves to a bowl with the crushed roasted peanuts and mix well.

Preheat the oven to 180°C/160°C fan/350°F/Gas mark 4. Remove the aubergines from the marinade, scrape off and discard the excess and warm the aubergines through in the oven for 10–15 minutes. Squeeze the lime juice over the warm aubergines.

To serve, arrange the aubergines in the centre of a bowl, glaze with the peanut sauce and pile on a generous serving of the curry leaf crunch. Garnish with the coriander leaves.

January King Cabbage, Shiitake and Baharat

The charred cabbage face is beautiful in this dish, after which it gets really well-cooked, so it becomes super juicy. It soaks up the braising liquor, taking on a texture that's rather like braised meat. In the restaurant, we serve this with butter, smoked over applewood, which adds some lovely floral, smokiness. It's not essential for the recipe, but if you want to try the smoking process at home, you can find instructions on page 22.

Serves 4

1 January King cabbage, tough outer leaves removed, hard bits of stem trimmed
1 tbsp rapeseed (canola) oil, for brushing
2 litres (70fl oz) Dashi Stock (see page 44; double the recipe)
Green Oil (see page 38), to serve

For the butter emulsion
½ tbsp double (heavy) cream
reduced dashi (see method)
80g (2¾oz) butter

For the shiitake chutney
40g (1½oz) dried shiitake
½ tbsp date molasses
½ tsp tamari soy sauce
½ tsp ground black pepper
2 tsp baharat spice blend
2 tbsp rapeseed oil
100g (3½oz) shallot, finely diced
1 tbsp plus 2 tsp sherry vinegar
1 heaped tsp demerara (light brown) sugar

Preheat the oven to 180°C/160°C fan/350°F/Gas mark 4.

Cut the cabbage in half horizontally, put in a roasting tin and brush the halves all over with the rapeseed oil. Heat the grill (broiler). When hot, grill the cabbage, turning, until blackened all over. Set aside.

Pour the dashi into the roasting tin, cover tightly with foil and braise the cabbage in the oven for 45 minutes to 1 hour, or until completely soft. Check with a knife: it should insert easily. Once cooked, strain 100ml (3½fl oz) of the dashi into a saucepan and simmer on a medium heat until reduced by half. Turn the oven down to a low temperature.

To make the butter emulsion, add the cream to the pan with the reduced dashi, then whisk in the butter. Set aside.

Meanwhile, for the shiitake chutney, put the shiitake in a bowl with the date molasses, tamari, black pepper, baharat and 250ml (9fl oz) of water and leave to soak for 1 hour. Once soaked, drain the shiitake (reserve the soaking liquid) and blitz to a coarse paste in a blender. Stir in the soaking water and set aside.

Heat the rapeseed oil in a pan over a medium heat and cook the shallot until translucent. Add the sherry vinegar and sugar, then simmer to reduce, until there is no liquid remaining. Add the shiitake mixture to the shallot pan and cook slowly, stirring, until reduced and dry, about 10 minutes.

To serve, warm the cabbage through in the oven, then dress generously the butter emulsion. Spoon the chutney into the base of a serving bowl and arrange the cabbage on top. Any leftover chutney can be kept covered in the fridge for up to 1 week. Dress the plate with more butter emulsion and drizzle with the green oil.

Börek

We created the spinach mix from this dish initially as a hot dip, but we couldn't quite find the right home for it. Then it tried its luck on a pizza collaboration that we worked on with the team from Yard Sale Pizza in London, to no avail, but it finally found a home wrapped up in filo – and here it is!

Before you start working with the filo, it's good to wet your hands – it will be much easier to shape each börek.

Serves 4

8 sheets filo (phyllo) pastry
100g (1¾oz) butter, melted
4 tsp House Za'atar (see page 40)
1 egg, beaten
1 tbsp runny honey, to serve

For the filling
1 tbsp olive oil
170g (6oz) leeks (2 medium), sliced, rinsed and chopped
170g (6oz) onion (about 1 medium), diced
600g (1lb 5oz) spinach
50g (1¾oz) dill, coarsely chopped
50g (1¾oz) sorrel leaves, coarsely chopped
4 tsp freshly grated nutmeg
100g (3½oz) Confit Garlic (see page 47), chopped
75g (2½oz) spring onions (scallions), chopped
zest of 1 unwaxed lemon
4 tsp cracked black pepper

For the whipped ricotta
150g (5½oz) feta
150g (5½oz) ricotta
½ tsp salt

For the filling, heat the oil in a large pan (use one with a lid) over a medium heat. Add the leek and onion and cook, stirring, until golden and caramelised, 10–15 minutes.

Add the spinach, cover with the lid and to allow the spinach to steam and wilt. This should take 3–5 minutes. Add all the other filling ingredients and stir to combine, then remove from the heat and set aside to cool.

For the whipped ricotta, put all the ingredients in a blender and blend on a high speed for about 1 minute until smooth. Set aside.

Preheat the oven to 190°C/170°C fan/375°F/Gas mark 5 and line a baking tray with baking paper.

To make each börek, lay a sheet of filo pastry so it is in portrait orientation on your work surface. Brush the surface with melted butter, then place a second sheet on top and brush again with butter. Spoon 75g (2½oz) of the spinach filling over three-quarters of the filo rectangle, leaving a 2cm (¾in) gap around the edges and a 5cm (2in) gap across the top.

Spoon the whipped ricotta along the bottom edge of the spinach. Working from the bottom edge, fold the filo over the ricotta and keep rolling the pastry up to form a cylinder, then form the cylinder into a snail shape.

Place the börek on the prepared baking tray, brush with beaten egg and dust with 1 teaspoon of za'atar. Repeat with the remaining filo pastry and filling to make 4 böreks. Bake for 25 minutes until golden brown and serve with a drizzle of honey.

Round Courgette with Brown Butter, Harissa Mayo and Pumpkin Seed Praline

The small, round courgettes (zucchini) are really firm and have delicate skins, but the yellow or green ones are interchangeable. The cooking liquor is also really tasty and makes a great base for a soup once you've finished with it. You can make the praline and zhoug ahead of time and they'll keep well in the fridge if you have any leftovers.

Serves 4

4 round courgettes (zucchini) (about 700g/1lb 9oz in total)
2 tbsp Harissa Salt (see page 43)

For the brown butter and harissa mayo
80g (2¾oz) butter
1 tbsp rose harissa
1 egg, boiled for 5 minutes, cooled and peeled
1 tsp Dijon mustard
1 tsp rice wine vinegar
½ tsp salt

For the coriander zhoug
25g (1oz) fresh coriander (cilantro)
10g (¼oz) parsley
2 tsp olive oil
1 tsp coriander seeds, toasted in a dry pan until fragrant
½ green chilli, deseeded and diced

Slice the courgettes in half and season the cut side with the harissa salt. Set aside for 1 hour, then scrape off the salt (discard). The salting process removes excess water and gives the squash a better texture. Set aside.

Meanwhile, for the brown butter and harissa mayo, melt the butter in a heavy-based a pan over a medium heat and cook, stirring until the butter has browned and smells nutty, about 5 minutes. When the butter is ready, stir in the harissa. Remove from the heat and allow to cool to room temperature.

In a blender, combine the egg with the mustard and vinegar and blend until smooth. Slowly add the butter mixture, blending well between additions, to form a smooth, emulsified sauce. Taste, season with salt and set aside.

For the zhoug, briefly pulse the coriander and parsley in a blender with the olive oil to roughly chop. Add the coriander seeds, then fold through the diced chilli. Set aside.

For the pumpkin seed praline, heat the oil in a pan. When hot, add the pumpkin seeds and fry until they are browned and starting to pop. Add the coriander and cumin seeds and the black pepper, then remove from the heat.

Recipe continued overleaf...

For the pumpkin seed praline

1 tbsp plus 2 tsp rapeseed (canola) oil
60g (2¼oz) pumpkin seeds
1 tsp coriander seeds
½ tsp cumin seeds
½ tsp black pepper
1 tbsp 1 tsp honey
½ tbsp white miso paste

For the braising liquor

5 tbsp plus 1 tsp olive oil
2 tsp coriander seeds
2 tsp fennel seeds
50g (1¾oz) rose harissa
450ml (16fl oz) white wine
140g (5oz) shallots, sliced
6 cloves of garlic, sliced
large pinch of chilli flakes
2 bay leaves
4 tsp caster (superfine) sugar
large pinch of cracked black pepper

In a separate small pan, heat the honey, stirring to prevent burning, until it caramelises. It will go light brown and start smelling delicious. Transfer the pumpkin seed mixture to a blender, then pulse the mixture, with the honey and miso, until it reaches a coarse praline texture. Set aside.

For the braising liquor, heat the olive oil in a pan and gently toast the coriander and fennel seeds, then stir in the rose harissa. Add the wine, bring to a boil and cook over a high heat for 2–3 minutes to burn off some of the alcohol (taste to check). Add 450ml (16fl oz) of water and all the other braising ingredients and bring to a simmer.

Poach the courgettes in a large pan with the braising liquor for 20 minutes, or until they are soft but still firm and holding together. Remove from the braising liquor and set aside, discarding the liquor.

To serve, spoon some of the pumpkin seed praline into each courgette half. Spoon the harissa mayo into a serving bowl and spread into a circle with the back of a spoon. Place the filled courgettes on top and spoon over the zhoug.

Delica Pumpkin, Hawaij Onions, and Pumpkin Seed Sambal

This dish celebrates the traditional Yemeni spice blend hawaij, which varies significantly by region – but at Bubala we make a mix of cumin, coriander, turmeric, black pepper and cardamom. The aromatic blend of spices works beautifully with the nutty flavour of the pumpkin (squash), which we accentuate with a pumpkin seed sambal of green chilli, garlic and lime. In the restaurant, we juice a butternut squash, but if you don't have a juicer, you can just double the carrot juice quantity, and the result will be just as delicious.

Serves 4

1 delica pumpkin (about 1kg/2lb 4oz)
salt and cracked black pepper
olive oil
1 tbsp confit garlic oil (see Confit Garlic, page 47), to serve

For the pumpkin glaze

4 tbsp plus 1 tsp butternut squash juice (see note, above)
4 tbsp plus 1 tsp carrot juice
1 tbsp pomegranate molasses
¼ tsp Hawaij Spice Blend (see page 42)
pinch of smoked paprika
pinch of salt

For the hawaij onions

2 tsp rapeseed (canola) oil
1 large (8oz) onion, finely sliced
10g (¼oz) fresh turmeric, thinly sliced into matchsticks
5g (⅛oz) fresh root ginger, thinly sliced into matchsticks
1 tsp Hawaij Spice Blend (see page 42)

For the pumpkin seed sambal

25g (1oz) onion
2 cloves of garlic
1 small green chilli
1 tbsp plus 2 tsp rapeseed oil
25g (1oz) pumpkin seeds
2½ tsp lime juice
¼ tsp flaky sea salt

For the pumpkin glaze, put the juices in a saucepan set over a medium heat and reduce by half. Transfer to a blender with all the other glaze ingredients and blitz to make a thick, sweet and sour mixture. Taste and add salt as needed. Set aside.

For the hawaij onions, warm the oil in a pan and add all the hawaij onion ingredients. Dampen and scrunch a rectangle of baking paper, then cut so it is the same circumference as the inside of the pan. Lay the paper directly on top of the onions (called a cartouche). Cook down slowly over a gentle heat until the onions are completely soft, 15–20 minutes. If the onions start to catch, stir in a splash of water and replace the cartouche. Set aside.

Meanwhile, for the pumpkin seed sambal, blend the onion, garlic and green chilli in a blender until it forms a smooth paste. Warm the oil in a pan, then add the paste along with the pumpkin seeds and cook slowly over a gentle heat until the rawness of the onion and garlic has gone, and the seeds start to toast, 5–10 minutes. Add the lime juice and salt and set aside.

To cook the pumpkin, preheat the oven to 190°C/170°C fan/ 375°F/Gas mark 5. Cut the pumpkin in half, from the stem to the core, and scoop out and discard the seeds. Cut each half in two, put in a roasting tin, toss in the olive oil and season with salt and pepper. Cover the tin tightly with foil to seal and roast for 30–40 minutes, or until fully soft through when tested with a knife. Heat the grill (broiler). When hot, put the pumpkin tin under the grill until the pumpkin skin is just charred. Brush with half of the glaze and keep warm in the oven until ready to serve.

Arrange the onions in a pile on a large plate and drizzle the remaining pumpkin glaze on one side. Sit the pumpkin on top of the onions and fill the cavities with about the sambal, then drizzle over the confit garlic oil.

Swede, Jalapeño and Burnt Apple with Curry Leaf Butter

Swedes are often overlooked – but we can assure you that slowly cooking in brown butter infused with curry leaf stalks transforms this humble vegetable into something spectacular. It takes on a deep, orange colour and becomes rich and indulgent.

We blacken the apples in the oven and blend to a ketchup-like consistency, then garnish the dish with a curry leaf and mustard seed temper.

You'll need to start the prep for the jalapeño shatta 3 days in advance. The leftover curry leaf brown butter is great to have in your fridge for cooking all sorts of things in.

Serves 4

2 large swede (rutabaga) (600–800g/1¼–1¾lb in total)

For the jalapeño shatta
100g (3½oz) jalapeños (4–5 medium)
2 tsp salt
1 tbsp cider vinegar
1 tbsp olive oil (more if needed, to cover the surface of the shatta)

For the burnt apple purée
200g (7oz) apples (about 2 small)
2 tsp caster (superfine) sugar
2½ tsp rapeseed (canola) oil
pinch of salt
2½ tsp cider vinegar

For the curry leaf brown butter
500g (1lb 2oz) unsalted butter
large handful of curry leaf stalks (reserve the leaves for the temper, overleaf)
pinch of salt

For the shatta, slice the jalapeños very finely, then sprinkle with the salt and transfer to a sealable plastic container. Leave in the fridge for 3 days.

After 3 days, drain the jalapeños, put in a blender with the vinegar, then pulse to a coarse paste. Transfer to a sealable container and pour the olive oil over the top. This will last for up to 3 months, covered in the fridge.

For the burnt apple purée, preheat the oven to 250°C/230°C fan/480°F/Gas mark 10. Line a baking tray with baking paper. Quarter the apples and toss with the sugar and 2 teaspoons of the oil. Lay the quarters on the lined tray, then roast for 45 minutes to 1 hour, until completely blackened. Set aside to cool.

Once cool, put the roasted apples in a blender with the cider vinegar, 2 tablespoons plus 1 teaspoon of water and the remaining ½ teaspoon of oil. Blend for 5 minutes to an emulsified, shiny purée that tastes savoury, sweet and acidic and has the consistency of ketchup. Set aside.

Reduce the oven temperature to 180°C/160°C fan/350°F/Gas mark 4.

Recipe continued overleaf...

For the temper
60g (2¼oz) reserved butter (from the swede; see method)
4 tsp yellow mustard seeds
2 sprigs curry leaves, leaves picked
½ tsp sherry vinegar

For the curry leaf brown butter, put the butter in a pan on a high heat and cook, stirring, until it foams and recedes, then takes on a hazelnut brown colour and has a nutty smell. This should take just a few minutes. Once it's ready, throw in the curry leaf stalks and salt, remove from the heat and allow to cool.

Top and tail the swede, then peel and cut in half. Place, cut-side down, in a small roasting tray (the pieces should fit snugly), and pour over enough of the curry leaf brown butter to cover them. Cover the tray with foil, seal well and roast for 2½ hours – turning the swede over halfway through – or until the swede has a deep orange colour and has started to brown on the bottom edges.

Turn the oven down to 140°C/120°C fan/275°F/Gas mark 1. Drain the swede, reserving 60g (2¼oz) of butter for the temper (store the rest), and return the swede to the oven to keep warm.

For the temper, warm the reserved butter in a pan until hot, then add the mustard seeds and heat until they start to pop. Throw in the curry leaves and cook until they crisp up. Remove from the heat, allow to cool slightly and stir in the sherry vinegar.

To serve, spoon the burnt apple purée onto a serving plate. Arrange the swede on the purée, top each with a teaspoon of shatta and spoon over the temper.

Calçot with Onion, Tarator and Egg

Calçots – sweet, charred spring onions – are celebrated in Catalonia, and here they get a Bubala spin. Layered with soft onions, creamy tarator, and a just-set egg, it's rich, smoky, and deeply comforting. A dish that lets onions, in all their forms, take the lead.

Serves 4

12 medium calçots
4 eggs
80g (2¾oz) Tarator (see page 39)
1 tbsp House Za'atar (see page 40)
pinch of flaky salt

For the leek molasses

100g (3½oz) green calçot trimmings (from calçots, above)
1 tsp vegetable oil
pinch of salt and cracked black pepper
pinch of brown sugar
4 tsp moscatel vinegar
1 tbsp rapeseed (canola) oil

For the leek and amba dressing

15g (½oz) green calçot trimmings (from calçots, above)
2 tbsp rapeseed oil
1 tsp amba (see page 34)

Rinse the calçots well and trim away any stray small roots, keeping the bases intact. Cut off the green parts of the calçots, dry them well and set aside.

For the leek molasses, chop the 50g (1¾oz) calçot trimmings into 7–8cm (3in) pieces. Bring a pan of water to the boil, add the trimmings and boil for 3 minutes, then scoop out and refresh in cold water.

Preheat the oven to 250°C/230°C fan/480°F/Gas mark 10 and line a baking tray with baking paper. Lay the blanched trimmings on the tray, drizzle over the vegetable oil, season with salt and black pepper and sprinkle over the brown sugar. Roast in the oven for 25 minutes, or until completely blackened, then set aside to cool.

Turn the oven down to 150°C/130°C fan/300°F/Gas mark 2. Prepare the barbecue for the calçots.

Once the trimmings have cooled, put them in a blender with the vinegar and 4 tablespoons of water. Blitz until completely smooth, then slowly add the rapeseed oil, blending until smooth and emulsified. Set aside.

For the leek and amba dressing, set a heatproof bowl over a bowl of ice. Put the 15g (½oz) calçot trimmings in a blender with the rapeseed oil and blend for 5 minutes, or until very smooth.

Recipe continued overleaf...

Transfer to a small saucepan over a high heat. Bring up to just below a simmer, then remove from the heat and strain through a sieve (sifter) lined with muslin (cheesecloth) into the bowl over the ice (the aim is to cool the oil down quickly to retain the colour). Once cool, mix the oil with the amba and set aside.

Bring a pan of water to the boil, then cook the eggs at a rolling boil for 7 minutes. Quickly scoop them out and run under cold water to stop them cooking further. When cool enough to handle, peel and set aside.

Roast the calçots on the hot barbecue, turning, until blackened on all sides. Let them cool on a baking tray covered with foil for 5 minutes, so they steam through. When cool enough to handle, peel away most of the blackened skins and put them in the oven to keep warm until you're ready to serve.

To serve, spoon a couple of piles of tarator onto a serving plate and, using the back of the spoon, make a small well and pour in a little of the leek and amba dressing. Spoon the leek molasses over the rest of the plate, add the calçots and dress with the remaining leek and amba dressing. Cut the eggs in half and nestle them into the calçots. Sprinkle over the za'atar and season with flaky salt.

SIDES & SALADS

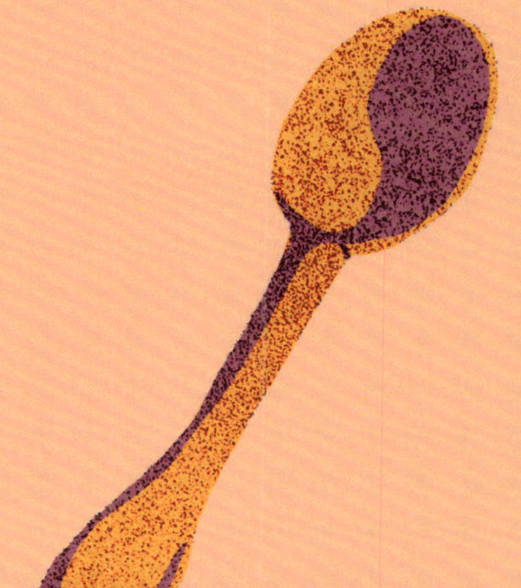

Cuore di Vesuvio Tomato with Basil and Tarator

Cuore di Vesuvio tomatoes are extremely fleshy and almost look like a melon when they're cut into. Their flavour is so concentrated that a drizzle of olive oil and a pinch of salt is all they really need. If you can't find them, use the biggest, ripest, juiciest tomatoes you can find. The tarator purée here is a bread-based emulsion that is reminiscent of taramasalata, and the tomatoes are fairly simply-dressed, with a sprinkle of capers and a few slices of shallot.

Serves 6

300g (10½oz) *Cuore di Vesuvio* tomatoes, quartered
1 tbsp capers, drained
¼ shallot, sliced
pinch of flaky sea salt
100g (3½oz) Tarator (see page 39)
handful of basil leaves

For the soy and rice wine dressing
4 tsp tamari soy sauce
2 tsp black rice wine vinegar
1 tbsp plus 2 tsp confit garlic oil (see Confit Garlic, page 47)

For the dressing, shake all the ingredients in a jar until well combined and emulsified. Set aside. Stir well and shake again before use.

To serve, put the tomatoes in a small bowl with the capers and shallot and season with the flaky sea salt. Spread the tarator on a serving plate, then pile the tomato mixture on top, finishing with the basil leaves and drizzling over the dressing.

Batata Harra

Our take on a Lebanese classic – these lemony, crispy, paprika-y potatoes are mega. They're first boiled, then crushed using the palms of your hands to create lots of small craggy areas that crisp up when fried. Make sure you toss the potatoes in the sauce at the very last minute to keep the potatoes as crispy as you possibly can.

Serves 6

900g (2lb) small waxy potatoes, such as new potatoes
rapeseed (canola) oil, for frying
2 carli peppers (about 90g/3¼oz in total), halved and sliced into 5–7cm (2–3in) pieces
½ tsp ground cumin
½ tsp table salt
1 tbsp lemon juice

For the dressing

1 clove of garlic
1 tsp aleppo chilli flakes
1 tsp merlot vinegar
2 tsp lemon juice
¼ tsp smoked paprika
4 tbsp plus 1 tsp rapeseed oil
a few sprigs of fresh coriander (cilantro), leaves picked
15g (½oz) parsley, leaves picked

For the dressing, put all the ingredients except the oil and herbs in a blender and blend to a smooth paste. Slowly add the oil, blending well between additions, until the dressing is smooth and emulsified. Add the herbs and pulse, so they retain some shape in the finished dressing. Season with salt and set aside.

Halve any larger potatoes so all the potato pieces are a similar size, if needed. Put them in a large pan of salted cold water, bring to the boil, then simmer for 10–15 minutes until just tender when tested with the tip of a knife. Allow to cool in the water. Once cool, crush the potatoes in your hands so that lots of craggy edges are exposed.

Heat 2cm (¾in) of rapeseed oil in a large, deep pan. When hot, fry the potatoes on all sides, turning, until all the edges and crannies are crispy, about 8 minutes. Do this in batches if needed. Drop the peppers in for the last minute. Scoop out and drain on a plate lined with paper towels, then toss with the cumin, salt and lemon juice.

Spoon the dressing into the bottom of a large bowl and pile the potatoes and peppers on top. Toss the mixture in the bowl to make sure the vegetables are thoroughly coated.

Mujadara

Mujadara is comfort in a bowl: humble lentils and rice transformed by deeply caramelised onions and warm spices. It's a dish that proves simplicity can be extraordinary, and it's ideal to serve when entertaining a group – double the recipe for a big crowd! A favourite from our 2020 Covid cooking classes on Zoom.

Serves 4

2 tbsp rapeseed (canola) oil, plus extra for frying
400g (14oz) Spanish onions (or other white onions), finely sliced
150g (5½oz) basmati rice
50g (1¾oz) beluga lentils
1 shallot, finely sliced
1 tsp coriander seeds
1 tsp cumin seeds
½ tsp ground cinnamon
½ tsp ground turmeric
10g (¼oz) fresh coriander (cilantro), chopped
sea salt and freshly ground black pepper

Gently heat the 2 tablespoons of oil in a large heavy-based pan, then add the onions and a pinch of salt, and cook, uncovered, on a very low heat, until really soft and golden. This can take up to 1 hour, so be patient and make sure to stir regularly so the onions don't stick and burn.

Meanwhile, rinse the rice and put in a pan (use one with a lid), adding cold water to cover so it comes 5cm (2in) above the surface of the rice. Add a pinch of salt, bring to the boil, then turn down to a simmer and cover the pan. Cook for 10 minutes, then turn off the heat and leave the rice, covered, for a further 10 minutes.

Cook the lentils in boiling, salted water until tender, then drain. In a small, separate pan, heat a splash of rapeseed (canola) oil and fry the shallot until crisp and golden. Remove with a slotted spoon and drain on a plate lined with paper towels.

Ten minutes before the end of the cooking time for the onions, add all the spices to the pan and cook, stirring regularly, until fragrant. After 10 minutes, add the cooked rice and lentils to the pan, stir gently to combine, then taste and check for seasoning, adjusting as needed.

Garnish with the crispy shallot and the coriander and serve.

Cuore di Vesuvio Tomatoes and Watermelon Salad with a Coconut and Lime Leaf sauce

As you can probably tell – with *Cuore di Vesuvio* featuring again in our recipes – these are our favourite tomatoes. The unusual combination of tomatoes and watermelon makes this salad completely refreshing. They work brilliantly together and are sure to blow people's minds!

Serves 4

250g (9oz) *Cuore di Vesuvio* tomatoes (2 large)
60g (2¼oz) peeled and prepared watermelon
small handful of basil leaves

For the coconut and lime leaf sauce
100ml (3½fl oz) coconut milk
5g (⅛oz) lime leaves
10g (¼oz) tamarind paste
3 tbsp date syrup
50g (1¾oz) coconut cream (from a solid block)

For the cumin dressing
½ tsp cumin seeds
1 small clove of garlic
¾ tsp moscatel vinegar
pinch of flaky sea salt
1 tsp agave nectar
¼ tsp orange flower water
1 tbsp rapeseed (canola) oil

For the coconut and lime leaf sauce, put all the ingredients in a pan and heat gently to reduce and thicken, 5–10 minutes. Strain, discarding the lime leaves, then taste to check the seasoning and set aside.

For the cumin dressing, toast the cumin seeds in a dry pan until fragrant, then grind in a mortar and pestle or spice grinder. Transfer to a blender, add all the other dressing ingredients, except the oil, and blend to combine. Slowly drizzle in the oil, blending until the dressing is smooth and emulsified.

To serve, cut the tomatoes and watermelon into 2.5cm (1in) chunks, put in a bowl and dress with the cumin dressing. Spoon the coconut and lime sauce into a serving bowl, pile the tomato and watermelon on top, and scatter over the basil leaves.

Potato Latkes with Toum

London-based restaurant critic Jay Rayner coined these the most inauthentic latkes ever seen. He's not wrong. These are inspired by the classics, served at the famous Quality Chop House in London, and they've been on our menu since our first-ever pop-up. We serve them with the mind-blowingly garlicky, Turkish condiment toum – which can really be paired with anything, if you have leftovers. These are the perfect side to any meal.

It's best to start this the day before you want to serve the latkes, as the potatoes need to be cooled and chilled before cutting.

Makes 12

800g (1lb 12oz) chipping potatoes such as Maris Piper or King Edward
125g (4½oz) unsalted butter
small handful of thyme leaves
3 cloves of garlic
1 tsp table salt
1 tsp crushed black peppercorns
rapeseed (canola) oil, for shallow frying
pinch of aleppo chilli flakes, to serve
pinch of flaky sea salt, to serve

For the toum
1 medium egg white
100g (3½oz) peeled garlic (about 30 cloves)
3 tbsp lemon juice
1½ tsp flaky sea salt
300ml (10½fl oz) rapeseed oil

Peel the potatoes and slice them very finely, using a mandolin, to a width of about 3mm (⅛in). Put in a large bowl.

Melt the butter in a pan, add the thyme leaves and garlic and leave on a low heat for about 10 minutes to allow the flavours to infuse. Remove from the heat, strain through a sieve (sifter), then pour the strained butter mixture over the sliced potatoes. Season with the salt and crushed pepper and mix until well combined. Set aside.

Preheat the oven to 180°C/160°C fan/350°F/Gas mark 4. Line a 40 x 30cm (16 x 12in) baking tin with baking paper, then add the potato slices in even layers. Cover with more baking paper and place a second baking tin, slightly smaller than the tin holding the potatoes, on top to weigh down the potatoes as they cook. Cook in the oven for 90 minutes, or until a knife passes through easily.

Cool, then transfer to the fridge and add heavy weights, such as full cans or jars, on top of the baking tin. Leave to chill until completely cold.

Meanwhile, for the toum, put the egg white, garlic, lemon juice and salt in a blender and blend until completely smooth. Slowly drizzle in the oil, blending well between additions, until the toum is thick, creamy and emulsified. Set aside. Any unused toum can be kept covered in the fridge for up to 3 days.

Turn the potatoes out of the tin. To portion the latkes, trim off the edges, then cut into 12 portions measuring about 5 x 8cm (2 x 3¼in) and 2.5cm (1in) deep.

Heat 1cm (½in) rapeseed oil in a frying pan (skillet) and, working in batches if needed, shallow fry the latkes until they are golden on both sides, 5–10 minutes. Transfer to a plate lined with paper towels to absorb the excess oil. To serve, stack the latkes on a plate, adding a generous dollop of toum alongside, and sprinkle with the aleppo chilli flakes and flaky sea salt.

Watermelon and Cucumber Salad with a Green Goddess Sauce

This salad plays on the well-known green goddess dressing, with a signature Bubala twist: tahini. One of our previous head chefs, Sara, put this dish on the menu a while back – it's a perfect summer salad.

Serves 4

10g (¼oz) Pickled Shallots (see page 50), to serve
140g (5oz) prepared watermelon, scooped with a dessert spoon into 4cm (1½in) pieces
urfa chilli flakes, to taste

For the marinated cucumber

125g (4½oz) cucumber, unpeeled
1½ tbsp salt
10g (¼oz) Preserved Limes (see page 49)
1 tsp agave nectar
pinch of flaky sea salt
1 tsp olive oil
2 tsp lime juice

For the green goddess sauce

1 tbsp picked mint leaves
2 tbsp picked parsley leaves
2 tbsp dill fronds
4 tsp lemon juice
50g (1¾oz) tahini
1 tsp agave nectar
pinch of table salt

For the marinated cucumber, thinly slice the cucumber into 1cm (½in) discs. Put the cucumber slices in a colander set over a bowl and toss with the table salt. Set aside for 1 hour to drain.

When the cucumber has finished draining, put the preserved limes in a blender and blend to a smooth paste. Transfer to a small jug and combine with the remaining marinade ingredients. Transfer the cucumber to a jar and pour the marinade over. Leave for at least 30 minutes before using.

To make the green goddess sauce, put the herbs, lemon juice and 3 tablespoons of water in a blender and blend until the herbs have completely broken down. The mixture will be very watery. Add the tahini and agave nectar and blend until smooth. The mixture should be quite thick now. Taste and season with salt. Set aside.

To serve, spoon the green goddess sauce onto a plate. Mix the marinated cucumber and pickled shallots together, stir in the watermelon, then pile them on top of the sauce. Season with urfa chilli flakes and a little extra flaky sea salt.

Jerusalem Artichokes, Ras el Hanout and Miso

Jerusalem artichokes are earthy, nutty, and just the right kind of weird – exactly the sort of ingredient we love at Bubala. Make sure you reach a good, golden brown colour when you're deep-frying them, as this is where the sweetness lies. They pair beautifully with the deep warmth of ras el hanout, and there's a hit of miso for unexpected umami.

This recipe makes more rosemary and ras el hanout salt than you need – it will keep in a sealed jar for up to 2 weeks.

Serves 4

300g (10½oz) Jerusalem artichokes, scrubbed
rapeseed (canola) oil, for frying and roasting
1 tsp salt
2 tbsp lemon juice, to serve

For the rosemary and ras el hanout salt
100g (3½oz) rosemary (about 2 bunches), leaves picked
50g (1¾oz) ras el hanout
20g (¾oz) flaky sea salt

For the miso sauce
35g (1½oz) white miso paste
30g (1oz) Confit Garlic (see page 47), about 6 cloves
½ clove of garlic
1½ tbsp lime juice
1 tsp Ras el Hanout (see page 42)
3 tbsp plus 2 tsp rapeseed oil

First make the rosemary and ras el hanout salt. Heat 2cm (¾in) of rapeseed oil in a heavy-based pan over a high heat. When hot, add the rosemary leaves and fry until crispy, then scoop out and drain on a plate lined with paper towels. When cool, transfer to a blender with the ras el hanout and salt and pulse to the texture of a coarse crumb. Set aside.

Preheat the oven to 225°C/215°C fan/435°F/Gas mark 7½.

Halve or quarter the artichokes lengthways, then toss with a drizzle of oil and the 1 teaspoon of salt. Spread evenly on a baking tray or shallow roasting tin, then roast in the oven for about 15 minutes, or until they are soft but not mushy. Once roasted, allow them to cool,

While the artichokes are roasting, make the miso sauce. Blend all the ingredients, except the oil, in a blender until thoroughly combined. Slowly pour in the oil, while blending, to form a thick emulsified sauce. Set aside.

To prepare the artichokes for frying, crush them between your hands, Heat 2cm (¾in) of oil in a large, heavy-based pan over a high heat. When hot, working in batches if needed, add the artichokes and shallow fry for about 5 minutes, or until golden brown and starting to crisp. Scoop out and drain on a plate lined with paper towels.

To serve, spread the miso sauce over a serving plate, pile the artichokes on top and season with the rosemary salt and lemon juice.

Gem, Shiso, Hazelnut and Apple

Gem lettuce, hazelnut, celery and apple feels like a pretty classic combination. We spiced up the hazelnuts and added a preserved lemon purée that adds a serious kick of salty sourness, giving the whole salad a lift. The celery pickle and hazelnut crumb can both be made ahead, and if you happen to have any pickle left over, it's a great addition to other salads or to eat with cheese.

Serves 4

½ apple
2 heads of baby gem lettuce
4 green shiso leaves, quartered

For the celery pickle
¼ head of celery (about 120g/4¼oz)
2 tsp coarse salt
160ml (5¼fl oz) rice wine vinegar
50g (1¾oz) caster (superfine) sugar
2 green shiso leaves

For the preserved lemon purée
45g (1½oz) Preserved Lemons (see page 49), pips (seeds) removed
1 tsp lemon juice

For the hazelnut crumb
30g (1oz) hazelnuts
½ tsp coriander seeds
½ tsp cumin seeds
½ tsp cracked black pepper
pinch of flaky sea salt

For the dressing
3 tbsp plus 1 tsp Green Oil (see page 38)
1 tbsp celery pickling liquor (from recipe above)

To serve
hazelnut crumb
preserved lemon purée
1 tablespoon celery pickle

For the celery pickle, slice the celery very finely (a mandolin is useful here) and put in a colander set over a bowl to catch any drips. Sprinkle with the salt and set aside for about 1 hour to drain. Meanwhile, make the pickling liquor by gently heating the vinegar and sugar in a saucepan, stirring until the sugar has dissolved.

Once the hour is up, squeeze out the excess liquid from the celery and give it a light rinse to remove the salt. Transfer to a heatproof bowl along with the shiso leaves. Reheat the pickling liquid and pour the hot pickling liquor over the celery and shiso. Set aside. This recipe makes more celery pickle than you will need. It will keep, covered in the fridge, for up to 1 week.

For the preserved lemon purée, blitz the preserved lemon and the lemon juice in a blender until smooth. Set aside.

For the hazelnut crumb, preheat the oven to 180°C/160°C fan/350°F/Gas mark 4. Put the hazelnuts on a baking tray and toast for about 15 minutes, or until they are a dark golden colour. Add all the other crumb ingredients to the tray, give it a shake to combine, then return to the oven for about 3 more minutes to lightly toast. Once cool, pulse lightly in a blender to combine, but leave very coarse. Set aside.

For the dressing, mix the green oil and the pickling liquor together, shake well before use. Set aside. Just before serving, thinly slice the apple. Dress the gem lettuce, shiso, apple and pickled celery with the dressing and a tablespoon of the crumb. Spread the preserved lemon purée around the base of a bowl, then pile the lettuce, shiso leaves and apple in the centre, creating lots of height. Spoon over the celery pickle and sprinkle more hazelnut crumb over the top.

Castelfranco, with Miso, Yuzu Kosho and Jerusalem Artichoke

Castelfranco's delicate bitterness plays off against the sweet, nutty artichokes here, with miso adding depth and yuzu kosho bringing a citrusy kick. It's a dish of contrasts – soft and crisp, rich and sharp – coming together in harmony. A little wild, a little refined, very Bubala.

Serves 4

1 head castelfranco, separated into leaves
1 head treviso, separated into leaves
1 head white chicory (endive), separated into leaves

For the yuzu and mustard dressing
15g (½oz) white miso paste
15g (½oz) Dijon mustard
½ clove of garlic
10g (¼oz) yuzu kosho
1 tsp lemon juice
1 tsp moscatel vinegar
½ tsp agave nectar
pinch of flaky sea salt
4 tbsp rapeseed (canola) oil

For the Jerusalem artichoke crumb
50g (1¾oz)Jerusalem artichokes, scrubbed
rapeseed oil, for shallow frying
¾ tsp Ras el Hanout (see page 42)
¼ tsp flaky sea salt

For the dressing, put all the ingredients except the oil in a blender and blitz to a smooth paste. Slowly add the oil, blending between additions, until the dressing is smooth and emulsified. Set aside.

For the Jerusalem artichoke crumb, finely slice the artichokes (a mandolin is ideal here). Heat 2cm (¾in) of oil in a frying pan (skillet). When hot, fry until the artichokes are golden brown. Scoop out and drain on a plate lined with paper towels and sprinkle with the ras el hanout and salt. Leave to cool, then pulse in a blender to form a coarse rubble texture.

To serve, dress the leaves with the dressing and arrange in a bowl, then sprinkle with the Jerusalem artichoke crumb.

Endive, Orange and Walnut

The dish comes out looking fairly unassuming, so we advise guests to dig deep and make little canapés for themselves. It's got everything for a great mouthful: freshness, fat, crunch, acid, and sweetness. All the elements can be made ahead and finished with the endive and grapefruit right at the end.

Serves 4

1 grapefruit, segmented, then segments sliced in half
3 heads white chicory (endive), trimmed, leaves separated

For the orange and amba purée
40g (1½oz) sugar
1 small orange, unpeeled
small thumb-sized piece of fresh root ginger, peeled and sliced
1 tsp amba (see page 34)

For the tamari caramel dressing
½ tbsp sugar
½ tbsp tamari soy sauce
small wedge of white onion
small thumb-sized piece of fresh root ginger, peeled and sliced
1 tbsp rice wine vinegar
½ tsp toasted sesame oil
½ tsp extra virgin olive oil

For the baharat granola
10g (¼oz) walnuts
1 tsp date molasses
1 tsp golden syrup
½ tbsp rapeseed (canola) oil
4 tsp linseeds
4 tsp sunflower seeds
pinch of flaky sea salt
pinch of baharat

For the orange and amba purée, bring 85ml (5 tablespoons plus 2 teaspoons) of water and the sugar up to the boil, then add the orange and the ginger. Turn down the heat and simmer for 2 hours with the lid on to stop too much water evaporating. Once cooked, the orange should be completely soft and almost falling apart. Allow to cool, then transfer the orange and ginger to a blender, adding 2½ teaspoons of the cooking liquid. Add the amba and blend until smooth. Set aside.

For the tamari caramel dressing, put the sugar and ¾ teaspoon of water in a small saucepan over a medium heat. Allow the sugar to dissolve, turning the pan from side to side so it cooks evenly. It is ready when it turns a dark treacle colour. When it's ready, take the caramel off the heat and add the tamari (be careful, as it may spit). Stir to combine, then remove from the heat and leave to cool.

Put the onion, ginger and half of the vinegar in a blender and blend until smooth. Pass through a sieve (sifter) into a bowl, discarding the remnants. Add the remaining vinegar and the sesame and olive oils. Once the tamari caramel is cool, mix that in too. Set aside.

Preheat the oven to 180°C/160°C fan/350°F/Gas mark 4. Line a baking tray with baking paper.

For the baharat granola, roughly crush the walnuts in a mortar and pestle or blender. Warm the date molasses, golden syrup and oil in a pan, then add the walnuts, linseeds and sunflower seeds, salt and baharat, and stir to combine.

Transfer to a baking tray and spread out in an even layer. Bake for 30 minutes, stirring every 10 minutes or so. Allow to cool and, if very lumpy, crush to the consistency of granola.

To serve, spoon the orange and amba purée into a serving bowl in an even layer. Lay out the grapefruit across the bottom of the bowl and add the granola. Cover with the chicory leaves, all facing the same direction, and drizzle over the tamari dressing.

Sweet Potato, Amba and Sunflower Tahini

Sweet potato brings the comfort, amba brings the punch, and sunflower tahini ties it all together with nutty richness. We love using the Yemeni spice blend Hawaij here. It all comes together in a sweet, tangy, creamy, and bold dish – a mix of flavours that shouldn't work, but absolutely does.

Serves 4

2 sweet potatoes (300–400g/ 10½–14oz in total)
2 tbsp vegetable oil
1 large or 2 medium onions (about 200g/7oz in total), sliced
table salt

For the sunflower tahini
110g (2oz) sunflower seeds, soaked overnight in water to cover
1 small clove of garlic
4 tsp lemon juice

For the hawaij emulsion
1 clove of garlic
1 tsp Hawaij Spice Blend (see page 42)
1 tsp amba (see page 34)
pinch of salt
1 tbsp plus 1 tsp rapeseed (canola) oil
1 tbsp chopped fresh coriander (cilantro) leaves

For the hawaij oil
2 tsp Hawaij Spice Blend (see page 42)
4 tsp olive oil

To serve
½ banana shallot, finely sliced into rings
a few sprigs of mint, leaves picked
a few sprigs of parsley, leaves picked
olive oil, for drizzling
pinch of Hawaij Spice Blend (see page 47)

Preheat the oven to 220°C/200°C fan/425°F/Gas mark 7. Bake the sweet potatoes for about 1 hour, or until they are soft all the way through when checked with a skewer.

Meanwhile, for the sunflower seed tahini, boil the soaked seeds for 1 hour until soft. Drain fully, then blend with the garlic, lemon juice and 2 tablespoons plus 2 teaspoons of water until smooth, with a consistency similar to tahini. This will take a few minutes. Set aside.

For the hawaij emulsion, in a pestle and mortar, crush the garlic, hawaij spice blend, amba and pinch of salt, until smooth. Slowly drizzle in the oil, working the mix until it's smooth and emulsified. At the end, add the coriander leaves and fold through. Set aside.

For the hawaij oil, mix the spice blend with the oil in a small bowl and set aside.

Heat the vegetable oil in a pan, then add the onions and season with salt. Cook on a medium heat for about 10 minutes, stirring, so they brown and caramelise fairly quickly, without turning mushy. Set aside.

To serve, slice the sweet potatoes in half and put on a serving plate. Dress each with the caramelised onions and spoon over the sunflower tahini and the hawaij emulsion. Arrange the shallot rings, mint and parsley leaves over the top. Finish with a drizzle of olive oil and the hawaij oil and a sprinkle of hawaij spice blend.

Beetroot and Blood Orange Fattoush, Black Garlic Tahini

Fattoush is a punchy, Levantine salad traditionally made with toasted flatbread and a sharp, herby dressing. We wanted to bring something new to it by adding roasted beetroot (beets), blood orange for brightness and crispy laffa through the salad – all on a bed of rich black garlic tahini.

Serves 4

5 tbsp coarse salt
2–3 medium beetroots (beets) (about 150g/5½oz in total), scrubbed
120g (4¼oz) pomegranate seeds
1 medium blood orange, segmented, then segments halved
1 small red onion, finely diced
½ red chilli, chopped
3 tbsp Black Garlic Tahini (see page 39), to serve

For the laffa crumb
120g (4¼oz) laffa flatbread
4 tbsp olive oil

For the dressing
1 tsp citric acid
1½ tsp merlot vinegar
pinch of sumac
pinch of aleppo chilli flakes
pinch of urfa chilli flakes
1 tbsp plus 1 tsp pomegranate molasses
1 tsp agave nectar
1 tbsp blood orange juice
1 tsp smoked paprika
pinch of table salt
6 tbsp rapeseed (canola) oil

For the herb mix
30g (1oz) parsley
15g (½oz) tarragon
15g (½oz) dill
20g (¾oz) mint

Preheat the oven to 200°C/180°C fan/400°F/Gas mark 6.

Scatter the coarse salt over a baking tray and place the beetroot on top. Cover the tray with foil and bake for 1 hour, or until the beets are fully soft when tested with a knife or skewer. Let them cool, then peel and cut into 1cm (½in) dice.

Meanwhile, slice the laffa into even pieces, put on a baking tray, toss in the olive oil and toast in the oven for 10 minutes. Remove and let cool a little, then either crush with a pestle and mortar or quickly pulse in a blender to form a coarse crumb. Set aside.

For the dressing, place all the ingredients, except the oil, in a blender and start to blend. After 20 seconds, begin adding the oil, drizzling it in slowly and blending between additions, until the dressing is smooth and emulsified. Set aside.

Just before serving, for the herb mix, finely chop all the herbs and mix together.

To serve, combine all the components, except the black garlic tahini, in a bowl until well incorporated. Taste for seasoning, adjusting as needed. Spread the black garlic tahini on a serving plate and pile high with the fattoush.

SWEETS

Baklava Semifreddo

This is Helen's riff on the classic dessert of Baklava: a version quite removed from the original, but one that still feels familiar when you're eating it. The beauty of a semifreddo is that it's essentially unchurned ice cream, so if you don't have a machine at home, it's a great alternative. You can also make it days in advance, so it's ideal for entertaining!

Serves 8–10

160g (5⅔ oz) egg yolks (from about 8 large eggs)
50g (1¾oz) caster (superfine) sugar
290ml (10fl oz) double (heavy) cream
1½ tbsp clear blossom honey
1 tbsp plus 2 tsp orange flower water

For the baklava nuts
85g (3oz) shelled pistachios
85g (3oz) halved walnuts
250ml (9fl oz) clear blossom honey
60g (2¼oz) white miso
2 tsp orange flower water
1 tsp flaky sea salt

For the cinnamon sherbet
70g (2½oz) caster (superfine) sugar
1½ tsp ground cinnamon
20g (¾oz) citric acid
scant tsp flaky sea salt

For the pâte de brick
rapeseed (canola) oil, for deep frying
8–10 pieces of pâte de brick, cut into 15cm (6in) triangles

Line a 900g (2lb) loaf tin with a double layer of cling film (plastic wrap), leaving enough overhang to close over the top.

In a large mixing bowl, use an electric whisk to beat the egg yolks and sugar together for about 10 minutes, or until very pale and creamy. The colour should be off-white.

In a separate bowl, using a hand whisk, beat together the cream, blossom honey and orange flower water to soft peaks. Be careful not to overwhip.

Gently fold the cream mixture into the egg yolk mixture, then pour into the lined loaf tin, covering the top with the cling film once filled. Put in the freezer for at least 8 hours, or ideally overnight.

For the baklava nuts, toast the pistachios and walnuts in a dry frying pan (skillet) on a medium heat until golden brown. Let them cool, then roughly blitz in a blender, leaving them fairly coarse and chunky. Mix the remaining ingredients in a bowl, then fold in the blitzed nuts. Set aside.

For the cinnamon sherbet, blitz all the ingredients together in a blender to make a very fine powder. Set aside. This recipe makes more cinnamon sherbet than you will need, so store the remainder in a sealed jar in a dry place for up to 2 weeks.

Recipe continued overleaf...

For the pâte de brick, heat some rapeseed oil in a heavy-based saucepan on a medium heat until it reaches 180°C (360°F). You can test this with a digital probe thermometer if you have one. If not, drop a piece of pastry into the oil and it should fizzle. Once hot, fry the pastry triangles for 30 seconds until crispy, then remove them from the pan, drain and dust with the cinnamon sherbet.

Slice the semifreddo using a hot knife, then serve each slice topped with a pâte de brick triangle, 1 tablespoon of the baklava nuts and a pinch of cinnamon sherbet.

Coconut Fudge

We serve these as a dessert option in our restaurant for guests who are too full for something bigger but still want a little something sweet. These petits fours also go beautifully with coffee. Unlike the cream in traditional fudge, the use of coconut here adds a delicious flavour, and has the added bonus of being vegan. See recipe photo overleaf.

Makes 40–45 pieces

320ml (11¼fl oz) coconut milk
320g (11¼oz) soft dark brown sugar
320g (11¼oz) caster (superfine) sugar
3 tbsp plus 1 tsp agave nectar
200g (7oz) coconut oil
2 tbsp orange flower water
1 tsp flaky sea salt
60g (2¼oz) tahini

For the sesame dusting

50g (1¾oz) black sesame seeds
50g (1¾oz) sesame seeds
50g (1¾oz) desiccated (dried shredded) coconut
pinch of flaky sea salt

Line a 24 x 20cm (9½ x 8in) baking tray with cling film (plastic wrap) and have your digital probe thermometer ready.

Put the coconut milk, both types of sugar, the agave nectar and coconut oil in a pan and bring to the boil. Reduce the heat to medium and keep swivelling the pan but don't stir, until the temperature reaches 116°C (240°F) degrees on a digital probe thermometer. It needs to reach at least 113°C (235°F) degrees to set, but it must not exceed 116°C (240°F), so keep a close eye on it (it may take 10–15 minutes). Once it has reached the correct temperature, take the pan off the heat and leave to cool until it reaches 43°C (110°F) degrees. During this time, do not stir the mixture, to prevent crystallisation.

Meanwhile, for the sesame dusting, lightly toast all the ingredients except the salt in a dry pan, then add the salt and combine.

Once the fudge has cooled, transfer to a mixing bowl and use an electric whisk to mix until the mixture has lost its sheen and turns matte, 2–3 minutes. Add the orange flower water and the salt at this stage, then continue to whisk until thick. This may take 10–15 minutes. The longer this beating process continues, the crumblier and better the fudge will be.

Once thick enough, stir in the tahini and press the mixture into the lined baking tray. Cover and leave to chill in the fridge overnight, then cut into 40–45 cubes. Coat with the sesame dusting to finish. Wrap any leftover fudge in baking paper and store in an airtight container for up to 1 week.

Photo overleaf...

Chocolate Truffles with Rose Cocoa Powder

Be warned, these creamy caramel truffles are highly addictive! The rose petal powder adds a beautiful, floral note that lifts the richness of the truffle. A match made in heaven. The recipe here makes about 45 truffles, so the perfect quantity for making and boxing up some as a gift – but we also can't be blamed if you eat the lot!

Makes about 45

300g (10½oz) caster (superfine) sugar
300ml (10½fl oz) double (heavy) cream
20g (¾oz) soft dark brown sugar
20g (¾oz) unsalted butter
½ tsp flaky sea salt
450g (1lb) chocolate, about 70% cocoa

For the rose cocoa powder
75g (2½oz) dried rose petals
250g (9oz) cocoa powder

Line a 24 x 20cm (9½ x 8in) baking tray with cling film (plastic wrap).

Put the caster sugar in a heavy-based pan and melt it over a medium heat until it reaches a dark caramel colour, about 7–10 minutes. Swivel the pan during this time but do not stir the sugar, to prevent crystallisation.

Once the sugar has turned to a dark caramel colour, remove the pan from the heat. Carefully pour in half of the cream. When the bubbles have subsided, add the rest of the cream and the brown sugar.

Stir gently to combine, then strain to remove any lumps. Stir in the butter and the salt to the strained mixture, then add the chocolate and allow to melt slightly before mixing.

Taste and add more salt if needed, then pour into the lined tray. Chill the mixture until set firm, ideally overnight.

Meanwhile, for the rose cocoa powder, blitz the rose petals to a fine powder and mix with the cocoa.

When the chocolate mixture has set, portion into 2–3cm (¾–1¼in) cubes. To finish the truffles, toss in the rose cocoa powder. Keep the truffles refrigerated and eat within 5 days.

Date and Tahini Ice Cream

Whether for breakfast on yoghurt or for dessert on ice cream, the combination of date molasses and tahini is the perfect balance of savoury and sweet. The ice cream here is flavoured with a date and tangerine jam, rippled through right at the end to bring a fruitiness that cuts through the cream.

Makes 1kg (2lb 3oz)

300ml (10fl oz) whole milk
300ml (10fl oz) double (heavy) cream
zest and juice of 1 scrubbed tangerine
150g (5oz) caster (superfine) sugar
150g (5oz) egg yolks (from 10 medium or 8 large eggs)
140g (5oz) dates, stones (pits) removed
tahini, to serve

First, make the custard for the ice cream. Combine the milk, cream and tangerine zest in a pan over a medium heat and heat until just steaming. In a mixing bowl, whisk the sugar and egg yolks together until pale and frothy.

Slowly add the milk mixture to the egg mixture, whisking continuously until fully combined, then pour the mixture back into the pan.

Heat very gently and stir continuously until the mixture reaches 83°C (180°F) when tested on a digital probe thermometer. If you don't have a thermometer, the custard is ready when it is thick enough to coat the back of a wooden spoon. Pour the custard mixture into a clean bowl, cover and chill.

Meanwhile, chop the dates and put them in a pan with the tangerine juice and cook over a gentle heat, stirring, until the mixture has thickened and has a jam-like texture. Set aside to cool.

Churn the custard mixture in an ice cream maker, following the manufacturer's instructions. When the ice cream is set, pour in the date and tangerine mixture and ripple through on its last few churns.

Serve with tahini drizzled over the top.

MOTHER MALABI

Supposedly, the original recipe for malabi was thickened with both ground rice and chicken, but we thought we'd avoid that for a veggie and vegan restaurant!

Our malabi is a coconut cream set with cornflour and seasoned with rose water. Once set, it's then whisked to create a decadent cream that we use as a base to pile other ingredients onto. Generally, this is a combination of some sort of granita, a nutty crunch and a syrup, all changing through the year. The result is that every spoonful has a bit of everything!

Serves 4–6 (Makes about 900g/2lb)

2 x 400ml (14fl oz) cans coconut milk
45g (1½oz) caster (superfine) sugar
30g (1oz) cornflour (cornstarch)
1½ tsp rose water

Set aside 100ml (3½fl oz) of the coconut milk in a bowl and pour the remaining 700ml (24fl oz) into a pan set over a medium heat. Add the sugar to the pan and bring to a boil, stirring to dissolve the sugar.

Meanwhile, whisk together the 100ml (3½fl oz) coconut milk and 5 teaspoons of water with the cornflour to make a paste, making sure there are no lumps.

Remove the coconut milk pan from the heat once the sugar has dissolved and whisk in the cornflour paste mixture until completely smooth. Return to a gentle heat to cook, whisking constantly until the mixture thickens, then stir in the rose water.

Cover and transfer to the fridge to cool overnight, or for at least 4 hours, then blitz in a blender until smooth before serving (see the recipes that follow).

Malabi, Red Grape, Rose Granita

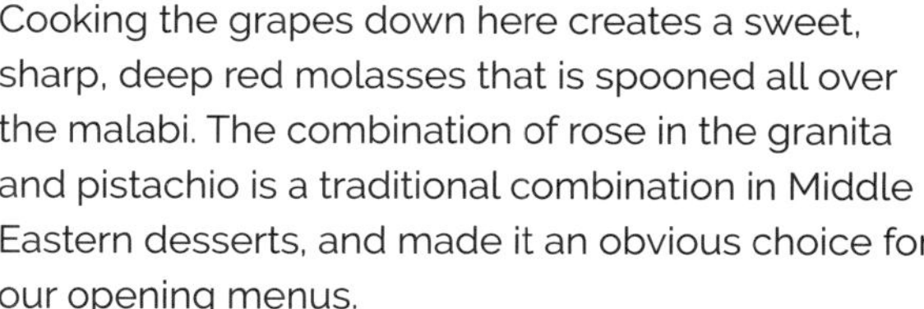
Cooking the grapes down here creates a sweet, sharp, deep red molasses that is spooned all over the malabi. The combination of rose in the granita and pistachio is a traditional combination in Middle Eastern desserts, and made it an obvious choice for our opening menus.

Serves 4

540g (1lb 3oz) Mother Malabi (see page 220), about half the full portion

For the red grape syrup

165g (5¾oz) seedless red grapes, stems removed
50g (1¾oz) soft dark brown sugar
¼ tsp black peppercorns
¼ star anise

For the rose granita

1¾ tbsp dried rose petals
30g (1oz) caster (superfine) sugar

For the pistachio crumble

60g (2¼oz) shelled pistachios with skins on
¼ tsp flaky sea salt
¼ tsp ground cinnamon
15g (½oz) icing (confectioners') sugar

For the red grape syrup, blitz the grapes in a blender until smooth, then strain through a sieve (sifter) lined with muslin (cheesecloth) into a pan and discard the solids.

Add the sugar, spices and 5 tablespoons of water to the strained grape liquid and cook on a medium heat until it reduces, thickens and forms a syrup, skimming the top to remove any foam. Test it's ready by putting a teaspoonful on a cold plate, refrigerating, then testing the consistency. If it flows easily, it's not quite ready, so cook for a bit longer. When it holds together and resists moving, it's there. Strain out the spices, cover and refrigerate.

For the rose granita, bring 140ml (4½fl oz) water to the boil in a pan. Add the rose petals and the sugar and leave to steep for 20 minutes. Transfer to a freezer-proof tub and freeze. Scrape with a fork every hour for 4 hours to create a loose, ice-crystal mixture.

For the pistachio crumble, preheat the oven to 160°C/140°C fan/325°F/Gas mark 3. Spread the pistachios out on a baking tray and roast for about 10 minutes, giving the tray a shake halfway through to turn them and stop them from sticking.

Let the pistachios cool, then pulse half of them in a blender to roughly chop. Set aside in a mixing bowl. Put the other half of the pistachios in the blender with the remaining crumble ingredients and blend for a few minutes until it forms a smooth paste, scraping down the sides of the blender as needed. It should have a tahini-like consistency, so add a splash of water if it's too sand-like. Transfer this paste to the bowl with the chopped pistachios and mix until thoroughly combined.

To serve, spoon the malabi into four separate bowls and drizzle with the grape syrup, top with the rose granita and sprinkle with the pistachio crumble.

Malabi, Sour Cherry, Peanut Brittle

Our red grape and rose granita malabi was our original version of this dessert, but as time went on, we felt we could play with the flavours a bit more, and this recipe is a riff on the classic combination of PB&J. The sour cherries add so much more to the 'jam', and the candied peanuts give a brilliant crunch of both savoury and sweet.

Serves 4

540g (1lb 3oz) Mother Malabi (see page 220), about half the full portion

For the peanut brittle

45g (1½oz) peanuts
85g (3oz) caster (superfine) sugar
½ tsp flaky sea salt
1 tbsp black sesame seeds

For the sour cherry syrup

35g (1¼oz) frozen sour cherries, defrosted
100g (3½oz) caster (superfine) sugar
1½ cinnamon sticks
½ star anise
2 tsp lemon juice

For the brittle, preheat the oven to 180°C/160°C fan/350°F/Gas mark 4 and line a baking tray with baking paper. Spread the peanuts over a second baking tray and roast for 5–10 minutes, or until golden.

Put the sugar and 5 teaspoons of water in a small heavy-based pan over a medium heat and cook until the sugar melts and turns a dark caramel colour, swivelling the pan from side to side so it cooks evenly, but making sure not to stir (this prevents the sugar from crystallising). Once it has turned a dark amber, add the roasted peanuts and the salt and sesame seeds and mix.

Quickly spread the peanut mixture evenly on the lined tray. Allow to cool and set firm, then break into rough pieces and pulse in a blender, working in small batches, until it has a coarse rubble texture. Set aside.

For the sour cherry syrup, put all the ingredients, except the lemon juice, in a saucepan with 300ml (10½fl oz) water. Heat on a medium heat, stirring to help dissolve the sugar, and reduce the mixture to a syrup. This will take about 10 minutes. When it has thickened to a honey-like consistency and coats the back of a spoon, it's ready.

Strain the syrup through a sieve, discard the spices and cherries and stir in the lemon juice.

To serve, spoon the malabi into four bowls. Drizzle with the sour cherry syrup and scatter over the peanut brittle.

Malabi, Clementine, Date, Sesame Brittle

This iteration of our malabi dessert came on the menu for our 2024 festive period and stayed until clementines were out of season, in the late winter. The dates, hydrated with cardamom, are a real grown-up treat, and the sesame brittle is based on the little sesame snaps you find on the counter of most corner shops.

Serves 4

540g (1lb 3oz) Mother Malabi (see page 220), about half the full portion
4 clementine segments, each cut into thirds

For the date syrup
35g (1¼oz) medjool dates
1 cardamom pod
⅛ tsp ground coffee
1 tsp date molasses
1 tbsp glucose syrup
1 tbsp demerara (light brown) sugar
small pinch of flaky sea salt

For the orange granita
250ml (9fl oz) orange juice
½ clove
scant tsp citric acid
¼ tsp salt

For the sesame brittle
4 tbsp sesame seeds
50g (2oz) caster (superfine) sugar
small pinch of flaky sea salt

For the date syrup, stone (pit) the dates, reserving the stones. Chop the dates and put in a heatproof bowl. Put the date stones and all the other date syrup ingredients in a pan with 3 tablespoons plus 1 teaspoon of water and heat gently until the sugar has melted. Pass through a sieve (sifter) and pour the liquid over the dates in the bowl. Stir well and allow to cool.

For the granita, blitz all the ingredients in a blender. Pass through a sieve, discard the solids, transfer to a freezer-proof tub, then freeze. Scrape with a fork every hour for 4 hours to create a loose, ice-crystal mixture.

For the sesame brittle, preheat the oven to 180°C/160°C fan/350°F/Gas mark 4 and line a baking tray with baking paper. Spread the sesame seeds over a second baking tray and roast until golden brown, 8–10 minutes.

Put the sugar and 2 teaspoons of water in a small heavy-based pan over a medium heat and cook until the sugar melts and turns a dark caramel colour, swivelling the pan from side to side so it cooks evenly, but making sure not to stir (this prevents the sugar from crystallising). Once it has turned a dark amber, add the sesame seeds and salt and mix.

Pour the sesame mixture onto the lined baking tray and allow to cool and set firm. Pulse in a blender to a coarse crumb, then set aside.

To serve, spoon the malabi into four bowls. Top each with 3 clementine pieces, a heaped tablespoon of the granita, a drizzle of date syrup and then scatter over the sesame brittle.

Chocolate Crémeux with Cacao Nib Salsa

A crémeux is rich, velvety chocolate set cream. We use a mixture of 100 per cent and 55 per cent chocolate and have spent lots of time searching for the best chocolate we can find to use here. The use of olive oil in the salsa adds some lovely floral notes, and the cacao nibs bring a satisfying crunch.

Serves 12

90g (3¼oz) egg yolks (from 5 large eggs)
360ml (12½fl oz) whole milk
360ml (12½fl oz) double (heavy) cream
130g (4½oz) caster (superfine) sugar
375g (13oz) chocolate, 55% cocoa
60g (2¼oz) chocolate, 100% cocoa
pinch of flaky salt, to serve

For the cacao nib salsa
35g (1¼oz) cacao nibs
5 tbsp olive oil
2 tsp date syrup
pinch of flaky salt

For the crémeux, first make a custard. Put the egg yolks in a mixing bowl. Put the milk, cream and sugar in a large heavy-based pan on a medium heat and whisk occasionally until the mixture just comes to the boil. Once the milk and cream mixture has reached boiling point, pour about one-third of the mixture onto the egg yolks. Whisk continuously to prevent the yolks from scrambling.

Once well combined, pour the custard back into the pan with the remaining milk mixture and put over a medium heat. It's really important to stir continuously to prevent the eggs from scrambling. If you have a digital probe thermometer, watch for the temperature to hit 84°C (183°F) and promptly take off the heat as soon as this temperature is reached. If you don't have a thermometer, the custard is ready when it is thick enough to coat the back of a wooden spoon.

Put both types of chocolate in a large mixing bowl and set a sieve (sifter) on top. Pour the hot custard through the sieve, directly onto the chocolate.

Discard the contents of the sieve, then whisk the mixture thoroughly in the bowl. Once the chocolate has melted and the mixture combined, pour into a 24 x 20cm (9½ x 8in) baking tray and use a spatula to smooth out and push into the edges of the tray. Cover with cling film (plastic wrap) and chill in the fridge until cool.

For the cacao nib salsa, combine all the ingredients thoroughly in a mixing bowl.

To serve, use a warm spoon to scoop out a generous dollop of crémeux and garnish with a spoonful of the cacao nib salsa and a sprinkling of flaky salt. Any leftover salsa can be kept in an airtight container for up to 1 week.

Chocolate Mousse, Banana, Tahini, Salted Caramel, Sesame Brittle

We created this centrepiece, Bubala's Big Pud, a sharing dessert for larger groups in our private dining rooms. It has a real wow factor when placed in the middle of the table, with jugs of tahini and caramel on the side to pass around. Nearly all the elements can be made in advance – ideal for minimal stress and maximum impact when entertaining. If you have a blow torch, brûléeing the bananas adds a little theatre, and a lot of flavour!

Serves 6

300g (10½oz) coconut cream
200g (7oz) chocolate, 100% cocoa
1 tbsp extra virgin olive oil
2½ tbsp glucose syrup
3½ tbsp date syrup
1 tsp ground cardamom
1 tsp flaky sea salt

For the sesame brittle
75g (2½oz) sesame seeds
125g (4½oz) caster (superfine) sugar
pinch of flaky sea salt

For the coconut caramel
150g (5½oz) caster (superfine) sugar
1½ tsp glucose syrup
90g (3¼oz) coconut cream

To serve
2 ripe bananas
caster (superfine) sugar, for brûléeing
60g (2¼oz) tahini

Chill the 300g (10½oz) coconut cream overnight in the fridge in a bowl set over iced water.

The next day, in a mixing bowl, whip the chilled coconut cream to soft peaks. Melt the chocolate with all the other mousse ingredients in a metal bowl set over a pan of simmering water. When melted and thoroughly combined, fold the chocolate mixture through the whipped coconut cream. Chill for at least 2 hours.

For the sesame brittle, preheat the oven to 180°C/160°C fan/350°F/Gas mark 4 and line a baking tray with baking paper. Spread the sesame seeds over a second baking tray and roast until golden brown, 8–10 minutes.

Put the sugar and 3 tablespoons plus 1 teaspoon of water in a small heavy-based pan over a medium heat and cook until the sugar melts and turns a dark caramel colour, swivelling the pan from side to side so it cooks evenly, but making sure not to stir (this prevents the sugar from crystallising). Once it has turned a dark amber, add the sesame seeds and salt and mix.

Quickly pour the mixture onto the lined baking tray and allow to cool and set firm, then snap into 8cm (3¼in) pieces. Set aside.

Recipe continued overleaf...

For the coconut caramel, put the sugar, glucose syrup and 2 teaspoons of water in a small heavy-based pan. On a medium heat, cook until the sugar melts and turns a deep golden brown colour and smells like toffee. This will take around 15 minutes. Keep swivelling the pan from side to side so it cooks evenly, but do not stir (to prevent the sugar from crystallising). Stir in the chilled coconut cream and allow the sugar to re-dissolve, then remove from the heat. Set aside.

To serve, spoon the mousse into the centre of a large bowl and spread to an even layer. Slice the banana lengthways into thirds and lay the slices over the mousse to completely cover. Sprinkle with an even layer of caster sugar and use a kitchen blow-torch to brûlée the top.

Serve the sesame brittle on a side plate, pour the tahini in a small jug and the caramel into another to pour over.

Bubalehs

These little ricotta doughnuts, that go by our namesake, are completely delicious when they've just been cooked and are still warm. They do need to be deep-fried for that perfect crunch, but if you're setting up a pan of oil for another dish, it's a great excuse to make these, too!

Makes 15

125g (4½oz) plain (all-purpose) flour
¾ tsp baking powder
625g (1lb 6oz) ricotta
75g (2½oz) egg yolks (from 4 large eggs)
100g (3½oz) egg whites (from 3–4 large eggs)
rapeseed (canola) oil, for shallow frying

For the fennel sugar
1 tbsp fennel seeds
1 tbsp caster (superfine) sugar

For the fennel sugar, toast the fennel seeds in a dry pan until fragrant – a couple of minutes will do. Roughly crush, keeping the seeds largely whole, in a pestle and mortar, then combine the fennel with the sugar in a small bowl. Set aside.

For the bubalehs, combine the flour and the baking powder in a large bowl, then add the ricotta and mix thoroughly.

Whip the egg yolks and whites in a stand mixer (or in a mixing bowl using an electric hand whisk) until airy and doubled in size, about 5 minutes. Gently fold the egg mixture through the ricotta mixture, cover, and chill for at least 4 hours. When chilled, transfer to a piping bag.

Heat a large, heavy-based saucepan with about 5cm (2in) depth of rapeseed oil to 180°C (360°F). If you don't have a digital probe thermometer, add a bit of batter to the hot oil. If it sizzles and browns, it's ready to go.

When the oil is ready, working in batches, use two spoons to shape small balls about the size of arancini, then place these gently into the hot oil and fry until golden brown. Give them plenty of space – they shouldn't touch each other as they cook. When cooked, they should look like little doughnuts. Remove with a slotted spoon, drain on a plate lined with paper towels and keep warm while you cook the rest. Sprinkle with the fennel sugar and enjoy.

Coconut and Cardamom Sorbet

Creamy coconut meets fragrant cardamom in this light, refreshing sorbet. It's simple, but the flavours are bold – sweet, spiced, and a little unexpected. A perfect palate cleanser or a standout finish. Serve in a dish that's as cold as possible!

Makes 1.5 litres (52fl oz)

1 litre (35fl oz) rice milk
400ml (14fl oz) tin full-fat coconut milk
1 tsp cardamom pods
1½ tbsp maple syrup
3 tbsp plus 1 tsp agave nectar
10g (¼oz) fresh root ginger
zest of ¼ unwaxed orange
a pinch of table salt
toasted desiccated coconut, to serve (optional)

Put all the ingredients into a large saucepan and simmer until reduced by half and really syrupy, about 15 minutes.

Leave to cool, then strain through a sieve (sifter). Transfer to an ice cream machine to churn and freeze, following the manufacturer's instructions.

Store in the freezer and use within 2 weeks.

When ready to serve, scoop out the sorbet into bowls and finish with a sprinkle of toasted desiccated coconut, if you like.

OUR SUPPLIERS

Ararat Bread

This hole-in-the-wall bakery on Ridley Road in Dalston, east London makes the best flatbreads you can get. I met Fizza, the stalwart behind Ararat, back in 2018, when we did our first pop-up. Fizza is special to me. She works night and day and has helped me out of the stickiest situations.

During the COVID lockdowns in 2020 and 2021, we were selling meal kits. One of our clients was running a one-off at-home film première event. We were supplying the breads and dips, and our client was packing it and sending it to VIPs. I got a call at midday to say 'The dips have arrived but when are the breads arriving?'

I'd forgotten to order the breads. I instantly called Fizza.

'Marc, the bakery is closed.'

'Fizza, I will never ask this of you again, but please could you make me 100 breads in the next 30 minutes.' And she did. She opened the bakery just for me and saved those VIPs from breadless dips.

When we only had one site, I would visit Fizza every Sunday to pay her weekly. No other supplier would demand these terms, but I loved it. She would always offer me a freshly made laffa wrap and wish me 'inshallah'.

132 Ridley Road
London E8 2NR

The Modest Merchant

I met wine merchant Al (Alex Percy) back in the pop-up days. He was just starting out, like me, and we formed a bond instantly. Al would come in person and sell his wines at our events, for no reason but to broaden everyone's knowledge of low-intervention wines and pass on his passion, which every customer felt. Al is a great man who has achieved incredible things in the wine industry and now sells his wines to some of the best restaurants in the UK.

themodestmerchant.com

Ren's Pantry

What can I say about spice supremo Ren? She's a force to be reckoned with and everyone in the industry knows her. Our team always mentions how amazing her training sessions are; she comes on-site to give tutorials, sharing her vast knowledge about spices. Ren's spices are incredible, and can't be beaten anywhere. You'll notice the difference between shop-bought and Ren's in all of our dishes.

renspantry.com

Other Suppliers we Love:

Natoora: natoora.com
All Greens: allgreens.co.uk
Belazu: belazu.com

In memoriam: Anthony Heard, Kupros Dairy

In 2023, I was heartbroken to find out that our cheese supplier, Anthony Heard, had passed away. He was in his early 30s. Meeting Anthony for the first time, at my flat in Dalston, was when I realized that the path I was taking was the right one. He turned up with a rucksack full of halloumi and feta for us to cook. We ate and chatted about cheese all afternoon. Anthony was the most passionate guy I have ever met. He knew everything about halloumi and feta and had created incredible versions of these cheeses. I'll never forget our first meeting and subsequent interactions. Anthony was a great guy and will forever be missed.

ABOUT BUBALA

Bubala is a love letter to the vibrant, spice-laden cooking of the Middle East – told through the lens of vegetables. Founded by Marc Summers, Bubala began in 2019 as a humble pop-up in London's East End before finding a permanent home in Spitalfields. It has since grown into a small family of restaurants, with locations in Soho and King's Cross, united by a bold and joyful approach to meat-free cooking.

Rooted in the flavours of the Middle East and beyond, Bubala reimagines the traditional by focusing on what's often overlooked: the extraordinary potential of vegetables. The name, a Yiddish term of endearment meaning 'darling', captures the spirit of the restaurants – welcoming, playful, and generous.

At Bubala, there are no meat substitutes or apologies for being vegetarian. Instead, the menus are built around dishes that stand confidently on their own – whether it's silky hummus with burnt butter, confit latkes with toum, or the now-iconic halloumi with black seed honey. Every plate is meant to be shared, every meal a conversation.

Bubala is not just about food – it's about the feeling that comes with it: comfort, discovery, and delight. This cookbook brings that experience into your kitchen, with recipes designed to be cooked, shared, and loved.

STAFF THANKS

Bubala is not just a restaurant. It's a feeling, a rhythm, a spark that exists only because of the people who bring it to life every day. Behind every dish, every service, every little detail that makes Bubala what it is, stands a team of remarkable individuals – passionate, creative, and endlessly dedicated.

To our chefs:
Thank you for cooking with your hearts, for pushing boundaries, and for treating vegetables like royalty. You've made our kitchens hum with energy and excitement without the unnecessary shouting that many kitchens still have.

To our front of house:
Your warmth, grace, and intuition are what make our guests feel at home. You don't just serve food – you serve joy, care, and welcome, every single time.

To our managers:
You are the calm in the chaos, the glue that holds everything together. Thank you for your tireless work, your resilience, and your ability to make the impossible look easy.

To our kitchen porters: Rotimi, Larry, Komi, Syed, Saheed, we see you. Bubala runs because of your unglamorous but vital work, and we are endlessly grateful.

This cookbook is a celebration of our food, yes – but it's also a celebration of you. The Bubala team is the soul of this place. This is your story as much as ours.

With Special thanks to:

Rosie Shennan:
For the huge amount of work, care and love that went into this book. I will be forever grateful.

Ben Rand:
Our Executive Chef, for bringing the recipes to life and making this book so special.

Support Team:
Lara, Sierra, Anu and Raj

Chefs:
Alexis, Amber, Vitor, Binney

General Managers:
Michael, Drew, Harriet

All Front of House and Back of House across Bubala past and present:
You make Bubala such a happy place to work and without you all there is no Bubala. I couldn't be prouder of the teams we have. You lead with kindness, empathy and compassion which is everything I could have asked for, and more.

BUBALA
BUBALA

ABOUT MARC

Marc Summers
Founder of Bubala

Marc Summers is the founder of Bubala, a celebrated collection of vegetarian Middle Eastern restaurants in London. Raised in Chigwell, Essex, Summers initially pursued a career in finance. However, his passion for food led him to change paths, gaining experience in kitchens in Australia before returning to the UK. Back in London, he worked at notable establishments such as The Palomar and Berber & Q, both as a chef and restaurant manager, where he developed a deep appreciation for Middle Eastern cuisine.

In 2018, Summers launched Bubala as a pop-up, aiming to showcase the richness of vegetarian Middle Eastern dishes. He opened the first permanent Bubala restaurant in Spitalfields in 2019.

Under Summers' leadership, Bubala has expanded to multiple locations, including Soho and King's Cross, earning acclaim for its innovative approach to vegetarian cuisine. His vision emphasises bold flavours and the celebration of vegetables without relying on meat substitutes, reshaping perceptions of vegetarian dining in the city.

THANK YOU

Sarah, Harry and Sadie
For being the best family and the reason behind it all.

Mum and Dad
For your unwavering support and belief.

Grandma Rose
For showing me what hospitality is meant to be and the name behind the restaurant.

Brothers Steve and Jon
For being my much older and wiser brothers and teaching me all I need to know.

Quadrille Team
For being the best publishers out there. Everyone in the team has been incredible, Stacey, Sophie and Kajal thank you!

Ben Clark
For being Bubala's biggest fan (And best book agent).

Shoot team; Patsy, Sammy, Luke, Tamara, Katie.
It was an unforgettable experience and brought the whole process to life.

Illustrations
Rory, you brought my vision to life with your brilliant illustrations – thank you so much.

Mattia and Josh
For giving me the opportunity to run their OG site, when no-one else would have let me. Gave me all the tools I needed.

Emilie Taillardat
for showing me the ropes and leading with empathy and compassion.

Emily Heron and Emily Herbert
For being the first chefs that believed in Bubala and collaborated on our first ever pop up.

Jake Norman
For being an all round top guy and best mate in the industry. Was there to get Bubala off the ground.

Helen Graham
For making Bubala what it is today. Without Helen we wouldn't be where we are.

INDEX

INDEX

INDEX

INDEX

INDEX

INDEX

INDEX

INDEX

BUBALA
OPEN
ENDLESS
8479

NOEL
STREET W1
CITY OF WESTMINSTER
POLAND
STREET W1
CITY OF WESTMINSTER
BUBALA

Quadrille, Penguin Random House UK, One Embassy Gardens, 8 Viaduct Gardens, London SW11 7BW

Quadrille Publishing Limited is part of the Penguin Random House group of companies whose addresses can be found at global.penguinrandomhouse.com

Published by Quadrille in 2025

www.penguin.co.uk

A CIP catalogue record for this book is available from the British Library

ISBN 978-1-83783-436-5
10 9 8 7 6 5 4 3 2 1

Managing Director, Publishing: Sarah Lavelle
Publishing Director: Kajal Mistry
Senior Commissioning Editor: Stacey Cleworth
Designer: Luke Bird
Design Manager: Katherine Case
Photographer: Patricia Niven
Props Stylist: Anna Wilkins
Food Stylist: Tamara Vos
Recipe Tester and Ghost Writer: Rosie Shennan
Recipe Developer and Ghost Writer: Ben Rand
Copy Editor: Susan Low
Proofreader: Wendy Hobson and Sarah Epton
Indexer: Beverley Winkler
Production Controller: Sabeena Atchia

Colour reproduction by F1

Printed in China by C&C Offset Printing Co., Ltd.

The authorised representative in the EEA is Penguin Random House Ireland, Morrison Chambers, 32 Nassau Street, Dublin D02 YH68.

Penguin Random House is committed to a sustainable future for our business, our readers and our planet. This book is made from Forest Stewardship Council® certified paper.